The Big Book of Presidential Trivia

Test your knowledge on the presidents:

Over 1,000 trivia questions

Compiled by

Cheryl Pryor

Arlington & Amelia Publishers

Author contact: nbaa@cfl.rr.com

ISBN-13:978-1886541108

ISBN-10:1886541108

FOR

DENNIS KAUS

WHO ALWAYS HAS AN ENCOURAGING WORD

TABLE OF CONTENTS

INTRODUCTION

This book is written in a format where you will have to turn to the end of each chapter to find the answers. The reason for using this format is so it doesn't ruin the fun if you're reading this on your own to test your knowledge. Too many times I've picked up trivia books where the answers are right below the questions which defeats the purpose.

This book is great for students, teachers, trivia buffs, or anyone wanting to learn more about the presidents or just testing what you already know.

If you enjoy this book be sure to look for The *'Big Book of First Ladies Trivia'* with trivia questions about the first ladies, their children, pets, homes, and the White House.

Presidents of the United States

1. George Washington 1789 – 1797

2. John Adams 1797 – 1801

3. Thomas Jefferson 1801 – 1809

4. James Madison 1809 – 1817

5. James Monroe 1817 – 1825

6. John Quincy Adams 1825 – 1829

7. Andrew Jackson 1829 – 1837

8. Martin Van Buren 1837 – 1841

9. William Henry Harrison 1841 – 1841

10. John Tyler 1841 – 1845

11. James Polk 1845 – 1849

12. Zachary Taylor 1849 – 1850

13. Millard Fillmore 1850 – 1853

14. Franklin Pierce 1853 – 1857

15. James Buchanan 1857 – 1861

16. Abraham Lincoln 1861 – 1865

17. Andrew Johnson 1865 – 1869

18. Ulysses S. Grant 1869 – 1877

19. Rutherford B. Hayes 1877 – 1881

20. James Garfield 1881 – 1881

21. Chester Arthur 1881 – 1885

22. Grover Cleveland 1885 – 1889

23. Benjamin Harrison 1889 – 1893

24. Grover Cleveland 1893 – 1897

25. William McKinley 1897 – 1901

26. Theodore Roosevelt 1901 – 1909

27. William H. Taft 1909 – 1913

28. Woodrow Wilson 1913 – 1921

29. Warren Harding 1921 – 1923

30. Calvin Coolidge 1923 – 1929

31. Herbert Hoover 1929 – 1933

32. Franklin D. Roosevelt 1933 – 1945

33. Harry Truman 1945 – 1953

34. Dwight D. Eisenhower 1953 – 1961

35. John F. Kennedy 1961 – 1963

36. Lyndon B. Johnson 1963 – 1969

37. Richard Nixon 1969 – 1974

38. Gerald Ford 1974 – 1977

39. Jimmy Carter 1977 – 1981

40. Ronald Reagan 1981 – 1989

41. George H.W. Bush 1989 – 1993

42. Bill Clinton 1993 – 2001

43. George W. Bush 2001 – 2009

44. Barack Obama 2009 -

1

Campaign Slogans

Answers are given at the end of the chapter.

Name the president whose campaign slogans are listed below

1. A Chicken In Every Pot And A Car In Every Garage

2. Change We Can Believe In

3. A Safer World And A More Hopeful America

4. Don't Swap Horses In The Middle Of The Stream

5. Happy Days Are Here Again

6. Tippecanoe And Tyler Too

7. Not Just Peanuts

8. For President Of The People

9. Hope

10. I Like Ike

11. Leave No Child Behind

12. Let Well Enough Alone

13. We Poked You In '44, We Shall Pierce You In '52

14. Kinder, Gentler Nation

15. He Kept Us Out Of War

16. Patriotism, Protection, And Prosperity

Answers

Chapter 1

1. Herbert Hoover

2. Barack Obama

3. George W. Bush

4. Abraham Lincoln

5. Franklin D. Roosevelt

6. William Henry Harrison

7. Jimmy Carter

8. Zachary Taylor

9. Barack Obama

10. Dwight D. Eisenhower

11. George W. Bush

12. William McKinley

13. Franklin Pierce

14. George H. W. Bush

15. Woodrow Wilson

16. William McKinley

2

Elections

Answers are given at the end of the chapter.

1. True or False.

Ulysses S. Grant's greatest asset, during his campaign for presidency, was that he was a war hero.

2. Who was the only president elected by a unanimous electoral vote?

3. True or False.

1848 was the first presidential election in which voting took place nationwide on the same day.

4. Which president won the Electoral College vote in one of the

closest and most controversial elections in America's history? It took over a month of recounts from Florida's voters. He was declared president, even though his opponent had more popular votes.

5. Which president helped fund his first political campaign from money he won playing poker while in the Navy?

6. Which president took his oath of office privately because of turmoil over his disputed election?

7. When this president ran for a second term he received 525 out of 538 electoral votes and carried 49 out of 50 states – *the largest number ever won*. Who was he?

8. **True or False.**

During the campaign for president, Ulysses S. Grant took no part in the campaign and made no promises.

9. **True or False.**

A large part of the reason Madison won his reelection was due to the fact that he passed out free whiskey to voters.

10. Which president's famous 'Checker's Speech' was his response to questions raised about gifts and money he received from

lobbyists?

11. Expecting to lose the election after the first returns came in, what president went to bed thinking he had lost the election? He ended up winning the election with the final count being 185 to 184.

12. Which president fought hard against illiteracy and poverty but is most remembered for his role in the Vietnam War?

13. Which president and vice-president never met until after their election?

14. Which president came within less than 100 votes to become the first president to ever be nominated for a third term?

15. Who was also running on the ballot for America's first president, other than George Washington?

16. Which president won his presidential election by 61% of the popular vote, the largest margin of victory in history?

17. Which president, when he was running for president, made the statement that he had campaigned in fifty-seven states with one state left to go?

Answers

Chapter 2

1. True

2. George Washington

3. True.

*This took place in the year 1848.

4.George W. Bush

5. Richard Nixon

6. Rutherford B. Hayes

7. Ronald Reagan

8. True

9. False.

*He lost his reelection in large part due to his refusal to pass out free whiskey.

10. Richard Nixon.

*He claimed the only gift he accepted was Checkers, a puppy for his daughter.

11. Rutherford B. Hayes

12. Lyndon B. Johnson

13. Taylor and Fillmore

14. Ulysses S. Grant

15. John Adams

16. Lyndon B. Johnson

17. Barack Obama

*That's right, he said fifty-seven states with one left to go.

3

What They Did Before And After Their Presidential Administrations

Answers are given at the end of the chapter.

1. Which president was a U.S. Minister to the Netherlands during one presidential administration, minister to Prussia during a different administration, and ambassador to the Russian court of Czar Alexander I during yet another administration, and then off to Great Britain, all before becoming president himself?

2. Before this president's inauguration took place seven states seceded from the Union. Who was he?

3. During his career in the Navy five of his seven years included submarine duty. Who was he?

4. Who was the only American president to have headed two branches of government – executive and judicial?

5. Which president was an inventor, and many of his inventions can be seen at his home today which is open to visitors?

6. Which president wrote nine of the ten amendments known as the Bill of Rights?

7. Who were the only two signers of the Declaration of Independence to become president?

8. He was in China during the Boxer Rebellion where he organized help for foreigners and years later when WWI began he helped Americans who were in Europe. This humanitarian, years later would also help Belgians after the intrusion of German troops. Who was he?

9. What was an occupation of George Washington before he became president?

10. Name at least one of the presidents who were awarded with the Presidential Medal of Freedom, the highest honor given to civilians?

11. Which president was an actor before he was president?

12. Before he became president he was promoted to general of the army. He was the first commander since George Washington to hold that rank. Who was he?

13. As a five year old child his father took him to visit President Grover Cleveland who told him, "I am making a strange wish for you. It is that you may never be president of the United States." Years later, that's exactly what he became. Who was he?

14. He ran the government like a political campaign, by always checking public opinion polls. Who was he?

15. Before he became president he served in the navy. His boat was rammed and he swam to safety and towed an injured man by his life jacket strap with his teeth. He scratched a message on a coconut shell to insure their rescue. Who was he?

16. Who served as President Jefferson's secretary of state?

17. What was an occupation of many of the presidents before they became president?

18. Which president worked as a fashion model?

19. Which president was selected as a delegate to the First Continental Congress in 1775?

20. As a state assemblyman he fought unsuccessfully to abolish a New York law requiring witnesses in court to swear belief in God. Who was he?

21. On an average he owned about two hundred slaves any given year. In his lifetime he freed only two of his slaves and only five more in his will. Who was he?

22. Which president, after he retired, went on an African safari and brought back plant samples and animals for the Smithsonian?

23. Which president was a school teacher before he was president?

24. Which president made a major contribution to the ratification of the Constitution by writing The Federalist Papers?

25. An Indian chieftain, Tecumseh, began an Indian confederation to prevent settlers from coming in and taking more of their land. This future president's troops killed Tecumseh and afterward the Indians scattered, no longer causing a serious threat. Who was he?

26. Which president was victim to a Wall Street scam leaving him

and his wife in financial ruin?

27. When he was in the Navy, one of the jobs of this future president was cleaning the toilets. Who was he?

28. Along with President Thomas Jefferson he established the Democrat – Republican Party. Who was he?

29. Which president was appointed Minister to the Netherlands by President George Washington, and was fluent in the Dutch language?

30. He was the only five star general to become president. Who was he?

31. He studied law under Thomas Jefferson who would become his mentor. Who was he?

32. Which president worked as a park ranger at Yellowstone National Park feeding the bears?

33. Which president designed his own home at Monticello and landscaped the grounds?

34. Which president was also a Founding Father, a vice-president to another president, and had a son who would also become president, and was also a descendant of Puritan colonists?

35. Which president was an accomplished pianist who played for a White House gathering when Kennedy was president?

36. He was the author of the Declaration of Independence. Who was he?

37. After completing his terms of president what work did George Washington do?

38. His work after his presidency earned him more respect than his presidential years. His later works include humanitarian works such as working with Habitat For Humanity. Who was he?

39. He co-wrote the Federalist Papers and sponsored the Bill of Rights. Who was he?

40. As an attorney he successfully represented a black woman who had been denied a seat on a streetcar. This case led to the desegregation of public transportation in New York City. Who was he?

41. Which president worked as a cattle rancher?

42. In his college days, which president was offered professional contracts with the Green Bay Packers and the Detroit Lions but turned them both down to study law?

43. He, along with the U.S. minister to France, actually approved and signed the Louisiana Purchase agreement. Who was he?

44. At one time he had to resort to selling firewood on the street to support his family. Who was he?

45. School officials considered this future president a discipline problem and went so far as to write to his father urging him to keep his son home. Who was he?

46. Who was George Washington's Secretary of State?

47. As a delegate to the Constitutional Convention in 1787, which president earned the title 'Father of the Constitution'?

48. Which president, after retirement, penned his memoirs while suffering from throat cancer so his wife would be financially stable?

49. He set the precedent for the dedication of post-term presidential libraries. Who was he?

Answers

Chapter 3

1. John Quincy Adams

2. Abraham Lincoln

3. Jimmy Carter

4. William Howard Taft

5. Thomas Jefferson

6. James Madison

7. John Adams and Thomas Jefferson

8. Herbert Hoover

9. Surveyor, military aide, soldier, or planter/farmer. Any of these answers would be correct.

10. Bill Clinton, Gerald Ford, George H.W. Bush

11. Ronald Reagan

12. Ulysses S. Grant

13. Franklin D. Roosevelt

14. Bill Clinton

15. John F. Kennedy

16. James Madison

17. Lawyer, farmer

18. Gerald Ford

19. George Washington

20. Millard Fillmore

21. Thomas Jefferson

* Each of these slaves were members of Sally Hemings family, a slave later proved through DNA testing, that he had children with.

22. Theodore Roosevelt

23. Lyndon B. Johnson

24. James Madison

25. W. H. Harrison

*Tecumsch was a Shawnee leader.

26. Ulysses S. Grant

27. Jimmy Carter

28. James Madison

29. John Quincy Adams

30. Dwight D. Eisenhower

*He retired to a home overlooking the battlefield at Gettysburg, Pennsylvania.

31. James Monroe

32. Gerald Ford

33. Thomas Jefferson

*He built into his house unique features such as: beds that retracted into a wall, a two-faced clock visible indoors and out, and a dumbwaiter.

34. John Adams

35. Harry Truman

36. Thomas Jefferson

37. He returned to farming at his home Mount Vernon.

38. Jimmy Carter

39. James Madison

40. Chester Arthur

41. Theodore Roosevelt

42. Gerald Ford

43. James Monroe

*He was sent to France by President Thomas Jefferson to help negotiate the sale of the Port of Orleans. Once arriving in France Monroe learned that Napoleon Bonaparte, to help finance his war in Europe, was willing to sell the entire Louisiana Territory. Not having time to seek presidential approval Monroe and Livingston (U.S. Minister to France) signed the agreement themselves. This doubled the size of the U.S.

44. Ulysses S. Grant

45. James Buchanan

46. Thomas Jefferson

47. James Madison

48. Ulysses S. Grant

49. Rutherford B. Hayes

4

Who Am I?

Answers are given at the end of the chapter.

1. The terrorist bombing at the Boston Marathon occurred during my presidency. Who am I?

2. During a battle I escaped injury, but my cloak had four bullet holes in it. I had two horses shot out from under me during this same battle. Who am I?

3. The collapse of communism in the Soviet Union occurred while I was president. Who am I?

4. I was president during the covert operation that led to the killing of Osama bin Laden. Who am I?

5. Electricity was installed while I was president. The First Lady was so terrified of it she left the lights on all night. Who am I?

6. I could write Greek with one hand while writing Latin with the other hand at the same time. Who am I?

7. I was the 10th president. Who am I?

8. I was the only president to resign. Who am I?

9. The beginning of America's worst financial crisis since the Great Depression began during my presidency. Who am I?

10. I was the 14th president. Who am I?

11. With the incumbent president standing unopposed for reelection there was no campaign. Not since George Washington had a president enjoyed such a broad based support. Can you name this president?

12. During my presidency suicide bombers killed over two hundred Americans when they attacked the Marine barracks in Beirut. Who am I?

13. This president introduced the Bill of Rights and the first ten Amendments to the Constitution. Can you name the president?

14. I lived in the Blair House, which is across the street from the White House, during most of my administration due to the fact that the White House was under renovation. Who am I?

15. As president I wanted to be the representative of the common man. Who am I?

16. I was the 2nd president of the United States? Who am I?

17. As a young boy he loved to read books about adventures and dreamed of one day becoming a sailor. As close as he would ever come to realizing that dream was to work towing barges up the Ohio Canal. Can you name the president?

18. Which president was looked upon as a traitor because he joined the Confederacy - he was the only president to have done so?

19. I was the 26th president? Who am I?

20. I am the grandson of the 9th president. I also became president. Who am I?

21. While I was president there was no vice-president. Who am I?

22. I married a widow with two children. I never had children of my own, but I adopted and raised her two children. Later in life I would also raise my two grandchildren. Who am I?

23. I am a direct descendant of William Brewster, the Pilgrim leader who arrived on the Mayflower. Who am I?

24. I was the 30th President of the United States. Who am I?

25. I banished alcohol from the White House. Who am I?

26. The 'Star Spangled Banner' became our national anthem while I was president. Who am I?

27. From the age of seven till the age of fifteen I was home schooled. Who am I?

28. After promising no new taxes in his presidential campaign he lost the support of many people when he did indeed raise tax revenues. Who was he?

29. His second term as president began with the worst financial

crisis in U.S. History. Who is he?

30. I was the 37th president. Who am I?

31. Included in his presidential library is a graffiti covered section of the Berlin Wall donated to him by the people of Berlin. Who is he?

32. Due to many of his promises and efforts, even though not fulfilled or lacking somewhat, he received the Nobel Peace Prize. Who is he?

33. I was the 13th President of the United States. Who am I?

34. I was one of the American diplomats sent to negotiate the Treaty of Paris which ended the Revolutionary War and recognized American independence. Who am I?

35. I only had a few months of formal schooling. Who am I?

36. He's considered by many to be the greatest president. Who is he?

37. As a teen, this future president received an appointment as an

official surveyor. Who is he?

38. I was the 29th president. Who am I?

39. I was fluent in seven languages. Who am I?

40. The Depression broke out while I was president. Who am I?

41. I was the 20th president. Who am I?

42. When I became president, at first I declined the salary Congress offered to me for the office of the president. I was already wealthy, and my desire was to serve as a public servant. Who am I?

43. I spoke to the public on the radio which were called "Fireside Chats." Who am I?

44. I was the 41st president. Who am I?

45. He was originally a liberal Democrat, but ran for the presidency as a conservative Republican. Who is he?

46. When I was a child I almost choked to death on a peach pit. My mother saved my life by forcing it down my throat with her fingers. Who am I?

47. I was the 18th president? Who am I?

48. He was the heaviest president in history weighing in at over three hundred pounds. Who was he?

49. I was the 39th president. Who am I?

50. His time of presidency was termed the "Era of Good Feelings." Which president was he?

51. I was the 19th president? Who am I?

52. These presidents were impeached by Congress, but not removed from office. Who were they?

53. I was the 34th president. Who am I?

54. I was the only twentieth century president who did not attend college. Who am I?

55. His presidency was the second shortest in history. Who was he?

56. I was the 32nd president. Who am I?

57. I was sworn in as president at my Washington hotel. Who am I?

58. When I was twenty years old my half-bother died of tuberculosis making me the head of one of Virginia's most prominent estates. Who am I?

59. I was the 33rd president. Who am I?

60. I was the son of Irish immigrants. Who am I?

61. I was the 3rd president of the United States. Who am I?

62. I was the 40th president. Who am I?

63. This president believed the president was 'a steward to the people' and that it was his place to take action for the good of the public. Who was he?

64. I was a five-star general. Who am I?

65. I was the 28th president. Who am I?

66. Who was the first president to be assassinated?

67. Who was the 22nd president and the 24th president?

68. I served on the First Continental Congress and helped draft the Declaration of Independence. I was a vice-president and a president. I earned a master's degree at Harvard. I was proved to be a patriot. I represented the British soldiers who were on trial for the Boston Massacre; even though others resented my decision to do so, I did this because of my strong belief that every person deserves a defense. Who am I?

69. I was the 11th president. Who am I?

70. He became president after being vice-president for only three months and after only meeting with the president a few times. Do you know who he is?

71. I was the 38th president. Who am I?

72. This president was described as kind and often helped people who were down on their luck. Who was he?

73. I was the 16ᵗʰ president. Who am I?

74. The spread of communism was a threat during his second term of office. Who was he?

75. I was the 8ᵗʰ president. Who am I?

76. I read the Bible daily, attended church regularly, and refused to discuss politics on Sunday. Who am I?

77. I was the 23ʳᵈ president. Who am I?

78. He was criticized for his slow response and not doing enough for the victims of Hurricane Katrina. Who was he?

79. I was the 5ᵗʰ president. Who am I?

80. He killed a man in a duel with a man who dishonored his wife. Who was he?

81. I was the 4th president. Who am I?

82. At one point this president had an approval rate of only 37% of Americans. Who was he?

83. During his presidency the U.S. enjoyed peace and economic well-being, more so than at any other time in history. Who was he?

84. I was the 21st president. Who am I?

85. Who was president during the 9-11 terrorist attacks?

86. I was the 31st president. Who am I?

87. At his inaugural, which president kissed the open Bible, which was turned to 2 Chronicles 1:10?

88. I was the 36th president. Who am I?

89. President Jackson described this president as a true man with no guile. Who was he?

90. I was the 35th president. Who am I?

91. I was the last president to keep a cow on the White House lawn. Who am I?

92. I was the 7th president. Who am I?

93. Not only was he the 23rd president, but the grandson of the 9th president. Who was he?

94. Which president enjoyed having friends to late dinners at the White House and afterward could be found taking a walk with his friends through the streets of Washington, sometimes as late as 3:00 or 4:00 AM?

95. I was the 25th president. Who am I?

96. This president wrote this in his diary on the day he left office: 'I feel exceedingly relieved that I am now free from all public cares. I am sure I shall be a happier man in my retirement than I have been during the four years I have filled the highest office.' Who was he?

97. I was the 6th president. Who am I?

98. It is believed this president may have had dyslexia. Who is he?

99. The stock market crash (of 1929) happened during his presidency which brought about the Great Depression. Who was he?

100. I was the 12th president. Who am I?

101. As a child he was angry when he was not allowed to go out with his older brothers, so he beat his hands against a tree. His mother explained the futility of being angry which he considered one of his most valuable lessons of his life. Who was he?

102. I was the 27th president. Who am I?

103. In the final year of his presidency the stock market plunged and the housing and banking industries were in a mess. Who was he?

104. This president believed in the power of prayer and proclaimed July 4, 1952 to be the first annual day of prayer. Who was he?

105. I was the 15th president. Who am I?

Answers

Chapter 4

1. Barack Obama

2. George Washington

3. George H.W. Bush

4. Barack Obama

5. Benjamin Harrison

6. James Garfield

7. John Tyler

8. Richard Nixon

*Why did he resign? He resigned rather than face an impeachment trial over Watergate.

9. George W. Bush

10. Franklin Pierce

11. James Monroe

12. Ronald Reagan

13. James Madison

14. Harry Truman

15. Andrew Jackson

16. John Adams

17. James Garfield

18. John Tyler

19. Theodore Roosevelt

20. Benjamin Harrison

21. Chester Arthur

*Why wasn't there a vice president? President Arthur assumed office at the death of President Garfield.

22. George Washington

23. Zachary Taylor

24. Calvin Coolidge

25. Rutherford B. Hayes

26. Herbert Hoover

27. George Washington

28. George H.W. Bush

29. Grover Cleveland

30. Richard Nixon

31. Ronald Reagan

32. Barack Obama

33. Millard Fillmore

34. John Adams or Thomas Jefferson, either or both is correct

*The Treaty of Paris negotiated between the colonies and Great Britain ended the Revolutionary War and recognized American independence. Five men had been commissioned to negotiate the treaty. These men were: John Adams, Ben Franklin, John Jay, Thomas Jefferson, and Henry Laurens. The negotiations were completed by John Adams, Ben Franklin, and John Jay. Henry Laurens had been captured en route by the British and Thomas Jefferson left the colonies too late to be a part of the negotiations.

35. Abraham Lincoln

36. Ronald Reagan

*This answer would also be correct if you said Washington, Jefferson, or Lincoln as they are also considered by many as being the greatest president.

37. George Washington

38. Warren Harding

39. John Quincy Adams

40. Herbert Hoover

41. James Garfield

42. George Washington

*Congress convinced President Washington to accept the salary in order to avoid giving the people the impression that only wealthy men could serve as president.

43. Franklin D. Roosevelt

44. George H.W. Bush

45. Ronald Reagan

46. Harry Truman

47. Ulysses S. Grant

48. William Howard Taft

49. Jimmy Carter

50. James Monroe

51. Rutherford B. Hayes

52. Andrew Johnson, Bill Clinton

* Richard Nixon resigned before he could be impeached, so you can't count him.

53. Dwight D. Eisenhower

54. Harry Truman

55. James Garfield

56. Franklin Roosevelt

57. Andrew Johnson

58. George Washington

* The estate was Mount Vernon

59. Harry Truman

60. Andrew Jackson

61. Thomas Jefferson

62. Ronald Reagan

63. Theodore Roosevelt

64. Dwight Eisenhower

65. Woodrow Wilson

66. Abraham Lincoln

67. Grover Cleveland

68. John Adams

69. James Polk

70. Harry Truman

71. Gerald Ford

72. Andrew Johnson

73. Abraham Lincoln

74. Harry Truman

75. Martin Van Buren

76. William Harrison

77. Benjamin Harrison

78. George W. Bush

79. James Monroe

80. Andrew Jackson

81. James Madison

82. Barack Obama

83. Bill Clinton

84. Chester Arthur

85. George W. Bush

86. Herbert Hoover

87. William McKinley

88. Lyndon B. Johnson

89. Martin Van Buren

90. John Kennedy

91. William Howard Taft

92. Andrew Jackson

93. Benjamin Harrison

94. Chester Arthur

95. William McKinley

96. James Polk

* He lived only three months after his retirement, the least of any former president.

97. John Quincy Adams

98. Woodrow Wilson

99. Herbert Hoover

100. Zachary Taylor

101. Dwight Eisenhower

102. William Howard Taft

103. George W. Bush

104. Harry Truman

105. James Buchanan

5

Presidential Quotes

Answers are given at the end of the chapter.

Name the president who is known to have said the statement below.

1. Which president quoted this statement: "If the rabble were lopped off at one end and the aristocrat at the other, all would be well with the country"?

2. "Change will not come if we wait for some other person, or if we wait for some other time. We are the ones we've been waiting for. We are the change that we seek."

3. "Those who dare to fail miserably, can achieve greatly."

4. "I have never been hurt by what I have not said."

5. "I know what I am fit for. I can command a body of men in a rough way; but I am not fit to be President."

6. "The Constitution is the guide which I never will abandon."

7. "In this present crisis, government is not the solution to our problems; government is the problem."

8. "We Americans have no commission from God to police the world."

9. "Never throughout history has a man who lived a life of ease left a name worth remembering."

10. "The friend in my adversity I shall always cherish most. I can better trust those who helped to relieve the gloom of my dark hours than those who are so ready to enjoy with me the sunshine of my prosperity."

11. "Speak softly, and carry a big stick."

12. "Trust, but verify."

13. A president whose term was ending said this to the president about to take his place as acting president: "My dear sir, if you are as happy on entering the White House as I am on leaving, you are a happy man indeed."

14. "Nothing can stop the man with the right mental attitude from achieving his goal; nothing on earth can help the man with the wrong mental attitude."

15. "Nobody will ever deprive the American people of the right to vote except the American people themselves, and the only way they could do this is by not voting."

16. "I know only two tunes; one of them is 'Yankee Doodle' and the other one isn't."

17. "There is power in public opinion in this country – and I thank God for it; for it is the most honest and best of all powers – which will not tolerate an incompetent or unworthy man to hold in his weak or wicked hands the lives and fortunes of his fellow citizens."

18. "Do I not destroy my enemies when I make them my friends?"

19. "When even one American who has done nothing wrong - is forced by fear to shut his mind and close his mouth – then all

Americans are in peril."

20. "Only if you have been in the deepest valley, can you ever know how magnificent it is to be on the highest mountain."

21. "The only man who makes no mistake is the man who does nothing."

22. "If anyone is crazy enough to want to kill a president of the United States, he can do it. All he must be prepared to do is give up his life for the presidents."

23. "Every immigrant who comes here should be required within five years to learn English or leave the country."

24. "Those who want the government to regulate matters of the mind and spirit are like men who are so afraid of being murdered that they commit suicide to avoid assassination."

25. "Prosperity cannot be restored by raids upon the Public Treasury."

26. "Let your heart feel for the afflictions and distress of everyone, and let your hand give in proportion to your purse."

27. "I am proud to be the first American president to come to Kenya – and of course; I'm the first Kenyan-American to be president of the United States."

28. "Believe you can, and you're halfway there."

29. "That government is best which governs the least, because it's people discipline themselves."

30. "Blessed are the young; for they shall inherit the national debt."

31. "Mr. Gorbachev, tear down that wall!"

32. "The most terrifying words in the English language are: 'I'm from the government, and I'm here to help.'"

33. "Never spend your money before you have earned it."

34. "Office holders are the agents of the people, not their masters."

35. "What I'd really like to do is go down in history as the president who made Americans believe in themselves again."

36. "I am not fit for this office, and should never have been here."

37. "Read my lips: No new taxes."

38. "A brave man is a man who dares to look the Devil in the face and tell him he is a Devil."

39. "We can't help everyone, but everyone can help someone."

40. "May God save the country, for it is evident that the people will not."

41. "The Constitution preserves the advantage of being armed which Americans possess over the people of almost every other nation, where the governments are afraid to trust the people with arms."

42. "A government big enough to give you everything you want, is a government big enough to take from you everything you have."

43. When Lincoln gave his acceptance speech on June 17, 1858 for the U.S. Senate he used the Biblical phrase: "A house divided against itself cannot stand." To what was he referring?

44. "Four-fifths of all our trouble in this life would disappear if we would only sit down and keep still."

45. "Enthusiasm for a cause warps judgment."

46. "Posterity! You will never know how much it cost the present generation to preserve your freedom! I hope you will make a good use of it."

47. "The truth is that all men having power ought to be mistrusted."

48. "A pessimist is one who makes difficulties of his opportunities, and an optimist is one who make opportunities of his difficulties."

49. "Worry is the interest paid by those who borrow trouble."

50. "Fighting battles is like courting girls. Those who make the most pretensions and are boldest usually win."

51. "Character is a journey, not a destination."

52. "You can put wings on a pig, but you can't make it an eagle."

53. "The less government interferes with private pursuits, the better for general prosperity."

54. "No person was ever honored for what he received. Honor has been the reward for what he gave."

55. "A president's hardest task is not to do what is right, but to know what is right."

56. "And so my fellow Americans, ask not what your country can do for you; ask what you can do for your country."

57. "I pray Heaven to bestow the best of blessing on this house," (referring to the White House) "and on all that shall hereafter inhabit it. May none but honest and wise men ever rule under this roof."

58. "Government's first duty is to protect the people, not run their lives."

59. "If government is to serve any purpose, it is to do for others what they are unable to do for themselves."

60. "In the end, it's not the years in your life that count. It's the life in your years."

61. "For time and the world do not stand still. Change is the law of life. And those who look only to the past, or the present, are certain to miss the future."

62. "It is far better to be alone, than to be in bad company."

63. "I do not like broccoli. And I haven't liked it since I was a little kid, and my mother made me eat it. I'm President of the United States, and I'm not going to eat any more broccoli."

64. "I stand for anti-bigotry, anti-semitism, and anti-racism."

65. "Any man who wants to be president is either an egomaniac or crazy."

66. "If you think too much about being reelected, it is very difficult to be worth reelecting."

67. "Better to remain silent and be thought a fool, than to speak out and remove all doubt."

68. "Don't pray when it rains, if you don't pray when the sun shines."

69. What president was President Thomas Jefferson referring to when he said: "_____ was so honest that if you turned his soul inside out, there would not be a spot on it."

70. "If you want to make enemies, try to change something."

71. "One of my proudest moments is, I didn't sell my soul for the sake of popularity."

72. This quote was spoken before this man became president, but nevertheless it is a statement that will go down in history attributed to this man. "No terms except an unconditional and immediate surrender can be accepted."

73. "It is not strange...to mistake change for progress."

74. "There are no adequate substitutes for father, mother, and children bound together in a loving commitment to nurture and protect. No government, no matter how well-intentioned, can take the place of the family in the scheme of things."

75. "You can fool all of the people some of the time, and some of the people all of the time, but you can not fool all of the people all of the time."

76. "We in America today are nearer to the final triumph over poverty than ever before in the history of any land."

77. "Within the covers of the Bible are the answers for all the problems men face."

78. "Always give your best, never get discouraged, never be petty; always remember, others may hate you. Those who hate you don't win unless you hate them. And then you destroy yourself."

79. "Our Constitution was made only for a moral and religious people. It is wholly inadequate to the government of any other."

80. "There is nothing stable but Heaven and the Constitution."

81. "I have always been afraid of banks."

82. "If anyone tells you that America's best days are behind her; they're looking the wrong way."

83. "That's all a man can hope for in his lifetime – to set an example – and when he is dead, to be an inspiration for history."

84. "Four score and seven years ago our fathers brought forth on

this continent a new nation, conceived in Liberty, and dedicated to the proposition that all men are created equal."

85. "Honest conviction is my courage, the Constitution is my guide."

86. "We will bring the terrorists to justice; or we will bring justice to the terrorists. Either way, justice will be done."

87. "Any man worth his salt will stick up for what he believes right, but it takes a slightly better man to acknowledge instantly and without reservation that he is in error."

88. "A man is known by the company he keeps, and also by the company which he is kept out."

89. "No tendency is quite so strong in human nature as the desire to lay down rules of conduct for other people."

90. "Those who deny freedom to others, deserve it not for themselves."

91. "To announce that there must be no criticism of the president, or that we are to stand by the president, right or wrong, is not only unpatriotic and servile, but is morally treasonable to the American

people."

92. "The only thing we have to fear is fear itself."

93. "Freedom is never more than one generation away from extinction. We didn't pass it to our children in the blood stream. It must be fought for, protected, and handed on for them to do the same."

94. "We did not come to fear the future. We came here to shape it."

95. "If you can't stand the heat, get out of the kitchen."

96. During his campaign for president he repeatedly told voters: "I'll never tell a lie."

97. "It takes a great man to be a good listener."

98. "I may be President of the United States, but my private life is my own damn business."

99. "It is easier to do a job right, than to explain why you didn't."

100. "Nobody cares how much you know, until they know how much you care."

101. "That's the good thing about being president, I can do whatever I want."

102. "No man will ever carry out of Presidency the reputation which carried him into it."

103. "I like the dreams of the future better than the history of the past."

104. "If Tyranny and Oppression came to this land, it will be in the guise of fighting a foreign enemy."

105. "Most folks are as happy as they make up their minds to be."

106. "Politics makes me sick."

107. "The surest way to win a war against poverty is to win the battle against ignorance. Even though we spend more on education than any other nation on Earth, we just don't measure up."

108. His last words were: "Oh, be good children, and we shall all

meet in Heaven."

109. "America will never be destroyed from the outside. If we falter and lose our freedoms, it will be because we destroyed ourselves."

110. "It's a recession when your neighbor loses his job; it's a depression when you lose yours."

111. "We can have no 50-50 allegiance in this country. Either a man is an American and nothing else, or he is not an American at all."

112. "Don't join the book burners. Do not think you are going to conceal thoughts by concealing evidence that they ever existed."

113. "It is my conviction that the fundamental trouble with the people of the United States is that they have gotten too far away from Almighty God."

114. "Do what you can, with what you have, where you are."

115. "As to the Presidency, the two happiest days of my life were those of my entrance upon the office and my surrender of it."

116. "We have a tendency to condemn people who are different from us, to define their sins as paramount and our own sinfulness as being insignificant."

117. "Be courteous to all but intimate with few, and let those few by well tried before you give them your confidence; true friendship is a plant of slow growth."

118. "Being president is like running a cemetery: you've got a lot of people under you and nobody's listening."

119. "One man with courage is a majority."

Answers

Chapter 5

1. Andrew Johnson

2. Barack Obama

3. John F. Kennedy

4. Calvin Coolidge

5. Andrew Jackson

6. George Washington

7. Ronald Reagan

8. Benjamin Harrison

9. Theodore Roosevelt

10. Ulysses S. Grant

11. Theodore Roosevelt

12. Ronald Reagan

13. James Buchanan said to Abraham Lincoln

14. Thomas Jefferson

15. Franklin D. Roosevelt

16. Ulysses S. Grant

17. Martin Van Buren

18. Abraham Lincoln

19. Harry Truman

20. Richard Nixon

21. Theodore Roosevelt

22. John F. Kennedy

23. Theodore Roosevelt

24. Harry Truman

25. Herbert Hoover

26. George Washington

27. Barack Obama

28. Theodore Roosevelt

29. Thomas Jefferson

30. Herbert Hoover

31. Ronald Reagan

32. Ronald Reagan

33. Thomas Jefferson

34. Grover Cleveland

35. Ronald Reagan

36. Warren Harding

37. George H.W. Bush

38. James Garfield

39. Ronald Reagan

40. Millard Fillmore

41. James Madison

42. Gerald Ford

43. Slavery

44. Calvin Coolidge

45. William Taft

46. John Adams

47. James Madison

48. Henry Truman

49. George Washington

50. Rutherford Hayes

51. Bill Clinton

52. Bill Clinton

53. Martin Van Buren

54. Calvin Coolidge

55. Lyndon B. Johnson

56. John F. Kennedy

57. John Adams

58. Ronald Reagan

59. Lyndon B. Johnson

60. Abraham Lincoln

61. John F. Kennedy

62. George Washington

63. George H.W. Bush

64. George H.W. Bush

65. Dwight D. Eisenhower

66. Woodrow Wilson

67. Abraham Lincoln

68. Richard Nixon

69. James Monroe

70. Woodrow Wilson

71. George W. Bush

72. Ulysses S. Grant

73. Millard Fillmore

74. Gerald Ford

75. Abraham Lincoln

76. Herbert Hoover

77. Ronald Reagan

78. Richard Nixon

79. John Adams

80. James Buchanan

81. Andrew Jackson

82. George H.W. Bush

83. William McKinley

84. Abraham Lincoln

85. Andrew Johnson

86. George W. Bush

87. Andrew Jackson

88. Grover Cleveland

89. William Taft

90. Abraham Lincoln

91. Theodore Roosevelt

92. Franklin D. Roosevelt

93. Ronald Reagan

94. Barack Obama

95. Harry Truman

96. Jimmy Carter

97. Calvin Coolidge

98. Chester Arthur

99. Martin Van Buren

100. Theodore Roosevelt

101. Barack Obama

102. Thomas Jefferson

103. Thomas Jefferson

104. James Madison

105. Abraham Lincoln

106. William Taft

107. George H.W. Bush

108. Andrew Jackson

109. Abraham Lincoln

110. Harry Truman

111. Theodore Roosevelt

112. Dwight D. Eisenhower

113. Warren Harding

114. Theodore Roosevelt

115. Martin Van Buren

116. Jimmy Carter

117. George Washington

118. Bill Clinton

119. Thomas Jefferson

6

Firsts

Answers are given at the end of the chapter.

I was the first president to...

1. Which sitting president was the first to own an iPod?

2. Who was the first president to host an Indian Chief in the White House?

3. Which president began the tradition of opening cabinet meetings with prayer?

4. Who was the first president to take oath of office in Washington, D.C.?

5. Who was the first president to marry while in office?

6. Who was the first president to have his oath of office administered by a woman?

7. What president built the first White House stables for his horses?

8. Who was the first president to travel outside the United States while president?

9. Who was the first, and only to date, Catholic president?

10. Which president was the first president to visit Alaska?

11. Who installed the first bathtub in the White House?

12. Who was the first president to have the oath of office administered aboard Air Force One?

13. Who was the first president to campaign by telephone?

14. Who was the first president to hold a press conference on television?

15. Which president was the first American to win the Nobel Peace Prize?

16. Who was the first president to appear on color television?

17. Who was the first president to have a Christmas tree in the White House?

18. Who was the first Democratic president since Franklin Roosevelt to win a second term?

19. Who was the first president to visit the West Coast?

20. Who was the first president to have a beard?

21. Who was the first president to be impeached, but was acquitted by one vote?

22. Who was the first president to travel underwater in a submarine?

23. Who was the first president to ride on a steamboat?

24. Who was the first "Baby Boomer" president?

25. Who became the first unelected president?

26. Who was the first president to engage in a televised debate?

27. Which president was the first to use an armored limousine?

28. Which president was the first to introduce the practice of group hymnal sings and prayer meetings at the White House on Sundays?

29. Who was president when the first annual Thanksgiving dinner took place at the White House?

30. Who was the first president to be outlived by his father?

31. What president, along with his wife the First Lady, installed the first library in the White House?

32. Who was the first president to visit China?

33. Who was the first president to own a radio?

34. Who was the first African-American president?

35. Who was the first president to live in the White House?

36. Which president was the first to ride on a train?

37. Who was the first president to voice support for same-sex marriage?

38. Who was the first president to play golf?

39. Who was the first president born an American citizen?

40. Who was the first president born west of the Mississippi River?

41. Which was the first president to exercise the pocket veto (by which a bill passed within ten days; excluding Sundays)?

42. Who was the first president to wear trousers or pants, rather than knee breeches?

43. Who won the first presidential race in which women were allowed to vote?

44. Who was the first Democrat elected after the Civil War?

45. Who gave the first presidential speech broadcast over the radio?

46. Who was the first president born outside the continental U.S.?

47. Who was the first president to ride in a car?

48. Who was the first president to have his face on a postage stamp?

49. Who was the first president to have his inauguration televised?

50. Who was the first president to have both parents see him become president?

51. Who was the first president to be a Rhodes scholar?

52. Who was the first president to have an official automobile?

53. Who was the first president to have a code name with the Secret Service?

54. Who was the first president to visit all fifty states?

55. Who was the first president to appear on television?

56. Who was the first president to run for office of the president against a woman?

57. Who was the first president to speak on the radio?

58. Who was the first president to have served in the U.S. Navy?

59. Who was the first president to die while in office?

60. Who was the first president to give a speech on television?

61. Who was the first president born in the twentieth century?

62. Who was the first president to visit Japan?

63. Who is the first president, and only to date, to earn a doctorate degree, PhD.?

64. Which president began the custom of flying the American flag from public buildings?

65. Who was the first president to invite a black man to dinner at the White House?

66. Who was the first president to have set eyes on the Pacific Ocean?

67. Which president was the first to be sworn into office outdoors?

68. Who was the first president to have his inauguration reported by telegraph?

69. Who was the first president to have nominated the first Jewish person to the U.S. Supreme Court?

70. Who was the first vice-president to succeed to the presidency after the death of his predecessor?

71. Who was the first president to be born in a hospital?

72. Who was the first president licensed to fly a plane?

73. Who was the first president, that previous to his election, was an actor?

74. Who was the first president to have his father visit him in the White House?

75. Who was the first president to speak for civil rights for African-Americans in the southern states and praised them for their service during WWI?

76. Who was the first president to be interviewed by a female reporter?

77. Though a few presidents have married women who had been divorced, who is the only president to date to have been divorced?

78. Who was the nation's first dark horse presidential candidate?

79. Who was the first president to call his home in Washington, D.C. the White House?

80. By the end of his presidency the nation reached from the Atlantic to the Pacific Ocean for the first time. Who is he?

81. While he was president the first telephone was installed in the White House. Who is he?

82. Who was the first president of the United States?

83. Who was the first president with a physical disability after being stricken with polio?

84. Who was the first Quaker president? (We've had two. Can you name them both?)

85. Who was president when the first Easter Egg Roll took place on the White House lawn?

86. Who was the first president to be born in the United States?

87. Who was the first president to be photographed?

88. Who was the first president who did not outlive his mother?

89. Who was the first president to have electricity in the White House?

Answers

Chapter 6

1. George W. Bush

2. Ulysses S. Grant

* While President Grant may have been the first president to host an Indian Chief, President Thomas Jefferson opened the White House to Sacajawea to visit previously.

3. Dwight D. Eisenhower

4. Thomas Jefferson

5. John Tyler

6. Lyndon B. Johnson

7. John Adams

8. Theodore Roosevelt

9. John F. Kennedy

10. Warren Harding

11. Millard Fillmore

12. Lyndon B. Johnson

13. William McKinley

14. John F. Kennedy

15. Theodore Roosevelt

* He won the Nobel Peace Prize for mediating peace between Russia and Japan.

16. Dwight D. Eisenhower

17. Franklin Pierce

18. Bill Clinton

19. Rutherford B. Hayes

20. Abraham Lincoln

21. Andrew Johnson

22. Harry Truman

23. James Monroe

24. Bill Clinton

25. Gerald Ford

26. John F. Kennedy

27. Franklin Roosevelt

*The limousine originally belonged to Al Capone, a gangster. The Secret Service needed a car to drive President Roosevelt to deliver his speech on Pearl Harbor the day after they were attacked. The

Treasury Department had impounded Capone's armored car years earlier so it was available for the president's use.

28. Rutherford B. Hayes

29. James Polk

30. Warren Harding

31. Millard Fillmore

32. Richard Nixon

33. Warren Harding

34. Barack Obama

35. John Adams

*He moved in the White House while the paint was still wet in November, 1800.

36. Andrew Jackson

37. Barack Obama

38. William Howard Taft

39. Martin Van Buren

*The previous presidents all were born prior to the Declaration of Independence so were born British subjects.

40. Herbert Hoover

41. Andrew Jackson

42. James Madison

43. Warren Harding

44. Grover Cleveland

45. Calvin Coolidge

46. Barack Obama

47. William McKinley

48. George Washington

49. Harry Truman

50. Ulysses S. Grant

51. Bill Clinton

52. William Taft

53. Harry Truman

54. Richard Nixon

55. Franklin D. Roosevelt

56. Ulysses S. Grant

*Virginia Woodhull, nominee of the Equal Rights Party ran against him.

57. Warren Harding

58. John F. Kennedy

59. William Henry Harrison

60. Harry Truman

61. John F. Kennedy

62. Gerald Ford

63. Woodrow Wilson

64. Benjamin Harrison

65. Theodore Roosevelt

*The first black man invited to dinner at the White House was Booker T. Washington.

66. Ulysses S. Grant

67. James Monroe

68. James Polk

69. Woodrow Wilson

70. John Tyler

71. Jimmy Carter

72. Dwight D. Eisenhower

73. Ronald Reagan

74. Millard Fillmore

75. Warren Harding

76. John Quincy Adams

*Ann Royall, a female reporter, had been refused an interview several times with President John Quincy Adams. She was aware that he regularly swam nude in the Potomac River so she went to the river while he was swimming and gathered his clothes and sat on them until she got the interview she had requested.

77. Ronald Reagan

78. James Polk

* A dark horse candidate is a candidate who is not well-known.

79. Theodore Roosevelt

*Prior to this time, the White House had been called the Executive Mansion or the President's House.

80. James Polk

81. Rutherford B. Hayes

*Alexander Graham Bell himself installed the telephone.

82. George Washington

83. Franklin D. Roosevelt

84. Herbert Hoover

*Herbert Hoover and Richard Nixon were both Quakers.

85. Rutherford B. Hayes

86. Martin Van Buren

*Up until this time the presidents preceding him were born in the colonies.

87. John Quincy Adams

88. James Polk

89. Benjamin Harrison

7

The One And Only

Answers are given at the end of the chapter.

The only president to have....

1. Who was the only president to win a Pulitzer Prize?

2. Who was the only president to have a foreign capital named after him?

3. Who was the only unanimously elected president by the Electoral College?

4. What president became both vice-president and president without being elected to either office?

5. Which president was the only man to serve both as president and as chief justice?

6. Who was the only president that served in both the American Revolution and the War of 1812?

7. Who was the only president that didn't represent a political party?

8. Who was the only former president to serve in the Senate?

9. Who was the only president to serve more than two terms?

10. Who was the only bachelor president in American history?

11. Who was the only president to serve in both WWI and WWII?

12. Who was the only president to serve two terms not in succession?

13. Who was the only president to take the oath of office from a female official?

14. Which president was the only man in history to hold the highest position in not only the executive branch, but also the judicial branch of the government?

15. Who was the only president to resign?

16. What president was considered to be a traitor for having joined the Confederacy? He was the only president to have done so.

17. What president is the only president to have been divorced?

18. Which is the only president to have been born in New York City?

19. Who was the only president to have been married in the White House?

20. Who was the only president elected to serve more than two terms?

21. Who was the only president to have no turnover in his cabinet?

22. Which president is the only president to have been elected as president four times?

23. What president was the only newspaper publisher to be elected president?

24. Who was the only president who had two assassination attempts against him made by women?

Answers

Chapter 7

1. John F. Kennedy

*He received the Pulitzer Prize for his biography, '*Profiles In Courage.*'

2. James Monroe

*Which capital was named after him? Monrovia in Liberia

3. George Washington

*James Monroe, the fifth president, received every Electoral College vote except for one. A New Hampshire delegate wanted to preserve the legacy of George Washington, and that is the only reason he didn't receive all the Electoral College votes.

4. Gerald Ford

5. William Howard Taft

6. Andrew Jackson

7. George Washington

8. Andrew Johnson

9. Franklin D. Roosevelt

*He served as President for over twelve years. He died shortly into his fourth term.

10. James Buchanan

11. Dwight D. Eisenhower

12. Grover Cleveland

13. Lyndon B. Johnson

* He took the oath of office aboard Air Force One following the assassination of John F. Kennedy with his wife present and the wife of John F. Kennedy, in her blood stained suit, beside him along with the body of John F. Kennedy aboard.

14. William Taft

15. Richard Nixon

16. John Tyler

17. Ronald Reagan

18. Theodore Roosevelt

19. Grover Cleveland

20. Franklin Roosevelt

21. Franklin Pierce

22. Franklin D. Roosevelt

*After he served as president, the Twenty-second Amendment was ratified in 1951 which limited the presidential office to two terms.

23. Warren Harding

24. Gerald Ford

8

Do You Know?

Answers are given at the end of the chapter.

1. How many presidents owned slaves?

2. Where was the capital of the United States first located? Hint: It's where President George Washington was sworn into office.

3. Before the Twelfth Amendment was passed in 1804, how was it determined who would be the vice-president?

4. Who was president when you were born?

5. Prior to the Capital Building in Washington, D.C., where were presidential inaugurations held? Which presidents were inaugurated there?

6. What agency is in charge of protecting the president and his family?

7. How were the two presidents Theodore Roosevelt and Franklin Roosevelt related?

8. What name was given to the commission established to investigate John F. Kennedy's assassination?

9. How many presidents have won the Nobel Peace Prize? Can you name them?

10. Which president was described as 'kind and often helped people down on their luck'?

11. Of all the presidents, which one lived the longest?

12. The tradition began of playing 'Hail to the Chief' to announce the arrival of what president due to the fact that he was so short that no one noticed when he entered a room?

13. Was Abraham Lincoln a Republican or Democrat?

14. Which two presidents are buried at Arlington National

Cemetery?

15. Who was the first president to marry while president?

16. Which two men, (both would become presidents), were running for the office of president and had to have the House of Representatives decide who would be the president?

17. Who was the youngest man ever **elected** to be president? How old was he? (There was a younger president who took office when the previous president was assassinated.)

18. What president hated political partisanship and felt that leaders should be able to discuss important issues without being bound by party loyalty?

19. Which president delivered the longest inaugural address, lasting one hour and forty minutes?

20. Which president has been voted our worst president?

21. Which president was the only preacher to become president?

22. Which president married a woman only to find out years later it

was invalid due to the fact that her divorce from her first husband had not become final?

23. Which president banned the sale of alcohol on Sunday?

24. Who was president when the Berlin Wall was taken down and East and West Germany were reunited?

25. Which president began the tradition of opening cabinet meetings with prayer?

26. Which president started the tradition of throwing out the first ball for the opening of baseball season?

27. What president donated his presidential salary to charity?

28. Which president couldn't read until he was nine years old?

29. Who was the oldest man to be inaugurated as president? How old was he at the time?

30. Which president read the Bible daily and refused to discuss politics on Sunday?

31. Who was the 12th president for just one day? (If you get this right, you can declare yourself a Presidential Genius!)

32. Which president was the last president of the Founding Fathers?

33. Before becoming president he was a sheriff, public executioner, and personally hung two murderers. Who was he?

34. After President Lincoln, who was the next president to be elected from the South?

35. He was the second president to also have a son who would become president. He also had another son run for the office of president. Who was he?

36. As an infant this president was once presumed dead by his parents who could find no vital signs after suffering from croup. They proceeded to put pennies over his eyes and drew a sheet over his face, when his uncle who was a doctor came in and revived him. Who was he?

37. Which president described himself as 'the most athletic president to occupy the White House in years'?

38. Which two presidents signed the Constitution?

39. Which president had studied to become a doctor?

40. What president was impeached, but was acquitted by one vote in the Senate?

41. Which president was the only president to elope?

42. Which president was the author of The Declaration of Independence?

43. Can you name one of the three reasons that would have been used for impeachment against President Nixon if he had not resigned?

44. Which president's heads are depicted on Mt. Rushmore?

45. Which president hated cats and after retiring would shoot at any cats that came near his home?

46. Which president wore black at all times in Washington, D.C.?

47. In warm weather which president went skinny-dipping in the Potomac early in the morning?

48. Which president had several inventions?

49. Which president was an indentured servant who ran away?

50. Which president often made his own breakfast in the White House?

51. Which president refused an honorary degree from Oxford, because he felt he had neither literary nor scientific achievement and didn't deserve the honor?

52. Who was president when the first annual Thanksgiving dinner took place?

53. The vice-president, Richard Mentor Johnson, took a slave for his common-law wife and raised and educated their mulatto children as free persons. Which president did this vice-president serve under?

54. What president is accused of chopping down a cherry tree and then confessing to the crime because he could not tell a lie? Sounds good, but this is a myth.

55. Which president dedicated the Statue of Liberty?

56. Which president studied nuclear physics?

57. During the Watergate scandal, what future president formally requested that Nixon resign from office?

58. Who was the first Republican to be elected to the Presidency?

59. What president talked to astronauts on the moon from the White House by using a radio-telephone?

60. Which president gave President Nixon a full pardon?

61. What president refused to use the telephone for presidential business?

62. Who was the tallest president? How tall was he?

63. Which president was accused of having African-American blood?

64. His approval ratings dropped significantly when it was found the IRS was targeting conservative organizations and also due to the cover up of the Benghazi terrorist killings. Who was he?

65. Which vice-president was visiting his father, when in the middle of the night he was informed that the president was dead? He was sworn in and then went back to sleep.

66. Who was the second president to be impeached?

67. Who is the only president buried in Washington?

68. Which president recommended eliminating the Electoral College?

69. Which president is the only president to have had his father administer the presidential oath of office to him?

70. What president never attended a single day of school?

71. Which president did not receive the news of his nomination for president because he wouldn't pay the postage due on the letter notifying him?

72. How many terms was Franklin Roosevelt elected?

73. Who was president when the journey of The Trail of Tears took place?

74. Which president, unsuccessfully, tried to have the words '*In God We Trust*' removed from money?

75. Which president started the custom of flying the American flag from all public buildings?

76. When his father split up the majority of his wealth among his children, what president declined his share, stating he didn't help earn it and therefore he didn't feel entitled to it?

77. Which two presidents died on the same day, the 50th Anniversary of the Declaration of Independence in 1826?

78. Which president could barely read or spell at the time he married his wife? She would later teach him to write and do arithmetic.

79. Although born with the first name Hiram a clerical error when he joined the military academy West Point enrolled him as another name, which rather than take the chance of not being enrolled in

the academy he changed his name. Who was he?

80. Which president was a bachelor until the age of forty nine?

81. Which president helped establish the Smithsonian Institute?

82. Who became president when President Nixon resigned?

83. Which was the last president born a British subject?

84. Which president sold his collection of books to the government which made up the foundation of the Library of Congress?

85. Which president remained unnamed for a month after his birth?

86. Which president wrote the book *Profiles In Courage* for which he won a Pulitzer Prize?

87. Which president worked at a peanut farm?

88. Which president married his teacher?

89. Which president never received a salary while president and even paid for all entertainment in the White House?

90. Which president wrote his own epitaph and never even mentioned that he had been president?

91. Which president served the shortest term of presidency?

92. Which president and his family had to live somewhere other than the White House when he first became president, as the White House had to be rebuilt after the British destroyed it?

93. Which president was so concerned about not wasting taxpayer's money that he went around the White House turning off lights that were not needed?

Answers

Chapter 8

1. Twelve presidents owned slaves at one time; eight of them while president.

2. New York City

*The capital was originally in New York City and later moved to the city of Philadelphia before moving to Washington, D.C.

3. The office of the vice-president was determined by the presidential candidate receiving the second largest number of electoral votes.

4. Answers will vary depending on the year you were born.

*Check in the front of the book where the presidents are listed in chronological order if you're not sure of your answer.

5. Federal Hall in New York.

*George Washington and John Adams were inaugurated in New

York. Thomas Jefferson was the first president inaugurated in Washington, D.C.

6. Secret Service

7. They were cousins.

8. Warren Commission

9. Four.

Theodore Roosevelt, Woodrow Wilson, Jimmy Carter, and Barack Obama

10. Andrew Johnson

11. Gerald Ford.

*He lived to be 93 years old.

12. James Polk

*Though the song was played for other presidents first, James Polk was so short it was used to announce his presence.

13. Republican

14. William Taft and John F. Kennedy

15. John Tyler

*His first wife died while he was president. He remarried while still in office.

16. John Adams and Thomas Jefferson. Also John Quincy Adams and Andrew Jackson.

17. John F. Kennedy was the youngest elected president at the age of 43. The youngest person to assume office was Theodore Roosevelt at the age of 42 after the assassination of William McKinley.

18. George Washington.

*He was unable to put a stop to political parties.

19. William Harrison

20. Warren Harding

21. James Garfield

22. Andrew Jackson

23. Theodore Roosevelt

24. George H.W. Bush

25. Dwight D. Eisenhower

26. William Howard Taft

27. Herbert Hoover

28. Woodrow Wilson

29. Ronald Reagan

30. William Harrison

31. Zachary Taylor for religious reasons did not want to be sworn

in office on a Sunday, and since President Polk's presidential term of office ended Saturday at midnight, the law required the office to be filled by the president pro tempore of the Senate, which was Davis Rice Atchison.

32. James Monroe

33. Grover Cleveland

34. Jimmy Carter

35. George H.W. Bush

36. Herbert Hoover

37. Gerald Ford

38. George Washington and James Madison

39. William H. Harrison

40. Andrew Johnson

41. John Tyler

42. Thomas Jefferson

43. 1- obstruction of justice   2- abuse of power   3- failure to comply with congressional subpoenas

44. George Washington, Thomas Jefferson, Abraham Lincoln, and Theodore Roosevelt

45. Dwight D. Eisenhower

46. Andrew Johnson

47. John Quincy Adams

*The last time he went skinny-dipping in the Potomac River he was seventy nine years old.

48. Thomas Jefferson

49. Andrew Johnson

*Many children from poor families were sold into indentured servitude. When he was twelve years old, he escaped from his master, a tailor in North Carolina.

50. Gerald Ford

51. Millard Fillmore

52. James Polk

53. Martin Van Buren

54. George Washington

55. Grover Cleveland

56. Jimmy Carter

57. George H.W. Bush

58. Abraham Lincoln

59. Richard Nixon

60. Gerald Ford

61. Calvin Coolidge

62. Abraham Lincoln at 6' 4".

63. Warren Harding

64. Barack Obama

65. Calvin Coolidge

66. Bill Clinton

67. Woodrow Wilson

68. Andrew Jackson

69. Calvin Coolidge

70. Andrew Johnson

71. Zachary Taylor

72. Four

73. Andrew Jackson

*The Trail of Tears was the removal of the Cherokee Indians from their homeland. Federal troops led some fifteen thousand Cherokees on a forced march from Georgia to Oklahoma. One out of four Indians died along the way.

74. Theodore Roosevelt

*He wanted the words removed because he said the money could be used for illegal or immoral purposes.

75. Benjamin Harrison

76. Ulysses S. Grant

77. John Adams and Thomas Jefferson

78. Andrew Johnson

79. Ulysses S Grant

*Ulysses was his middle name and the S stood for Simpson, his mother's maiden name, the clerk at the school believed. Not wanting problems with his enrollment into West Point Academy he changed his name – though he said the S didn't stand for anything; though he was quite pleased with the initials U.S.

80. Grover Cleveland

81. John Quincy Adams

82. Gerald Ford

83. William Henry Harrison

84. Thomas Jefferson

85. Ulysses S. Grant

*His middle name, Ulysses was after a hero of Greek mythology.

86. John F. Kennedy

*It was later said that the book was more the work of his aide Theodore Sorenson than that of Kennedy himself.

87. Jimmy Carter

88. Millard Fillmore

89. Herbert Hoover

90. Thomas Jefferson

91. William H. Harrison

*He died thirty two days after elected. His inaugural address lasted almost two hours in which time he stood in the bad weather wearing no hat or coat. After his inaugural address he attended a round of receptions in his wet clothing and developed a chill which within days turned into a cold and then progressed into pneumonia. One month after taking office he passed away.

92. James Monroe

*They lived in a house on I Street in Washington, D.C. They later moved into the White House.

93. Lyndon B. Johnson

9

Achievements

Answers are given at the end of the chapter.

What president is responsible for these achievements...

1. What president gave the Star Wars speech about the Strategic Defense Initiative, also known as SDI?

2. Which president was responsible for keeping the Union intact?

3. Which president signed the treaty to purchase Alaska from Russia?

4. Which president had the lowest government spending in thirty years?

5. Who was president during the ratification of the Seventeenth Amendment?

6. Which president passed Health Care Reform?

7. Which president put an end to the problem of Barbary pirates by deploying warships?

8. Who was president when the first national Mother's Day was proclaimed?

9. Which president visited both China and the Soviet Union to reduce tensions between these countries and the United States? These visits helped establish diplomatic relations.

10. Which president created the departments: Department of Energy and the Department of Education?

11. Which president was responsible for deactivating more than 1,700 nuclear warheads from the former Soviet Union?

12. Which president vetoed a bill that banned Chinese immigrants from entering the United States?

13. Which president ended the war in Iraq?

14. Which president helped reduce tensions with the Soviet Union when he signed the Helsinki Accords?

15. Which president signed the first child welfare program?

16. Which president founded the Environmental Protection Agency?

17. Which president signed the Civil Rights Act that extended the rights of emancipated slaves?

18. Which president issued the Emancipation Proclamation?

19. Which president established federal protection for national parks, forests, and national monuments?

20. Which president signed the Civil Rights Acts of 1964 and 1968?

21. Which president's greatest accomplishment as president was a strong economy?

22. Which president reasserted the superiority of the president on the issue of executive appointments?

23. Which president ended the Korean War?

24. Which president was instrumental in securing passage of the Religious Freedom Statute?

25. Which president had some of his greatest achievements in the area of conservation?

26. Which president created programs to tackle poverty such as: Head Start, food stamps, Medicare, and Medicaid?

27. Which president signed the Nineteenth Amendment granting women the right to vote?

28. Which president, one of the last acts of his presidency, had a civil rights bill passed as the landmark Civil Rights Act in 1964?

29. Which president lowered the voting age from twenty-one years to eighteen years?

30. Which president significantly lowered tax rates for nearly all

U.S. Tax payers?

31. Which president achieved a major victory when the House of Representatives approved a bipartisan agreement on tax increases and spending cuts?

32. Who was president when Congress passed the Embargo Act of 1807 which prohibited American ships from trading in all foreign ports?

33. Which president signed The Missouri Compromise?

34. Which president signed the Paris Peace Accords ending U.S. involvement in the Vietnam War?

35. Which president issued the doctrine that would contain communism?

36. Who was president when the Cold War ended?

37. Which president fulfilled every single one of his campaign promises while serving only one term of office?

38. Which president prevented annexation of Cuba?

39. Which president prevented nuclear Armageddon?

40. Which president was responsible for the Monroe Doctrine?

41. Which president helped restore the public's confidence in government after the Watergate scandal?

42. Which president's handling of the invasion in Kuwait is looked upon as his greatest presidential success?

43. Which president built up the U.S. Navy?

44. Who was president when the Louisiana Purchase came about?

45. Which president balanced the budget – not just once; but three times?

46. Which president promoted public works such as the Hoover Dam?

47. With the Oregon Treaty of 1846, this president acquired a substantial amount of land for the U.S. from the British without having to go to war to do so. Who was he?

48. Which president established the Peace Corps?

49. Which president joined with Mexico to strengthen border security?

50. Which president oversaw desegregation peacefully of the schools in the South?

51. Which president established the Open Door policy with China?

52. Which president officially ended the U.S. involvement in the Vietnam War?

53. Which president's proudest accomplishment was the Virginia Statute for Religious Freedom?

54. Which president kept America at peace, even though he was faced with major Cold War issues every year he was in office?

55. Which president established Social Security?

56. Which president was responsible for eliminating Osama bin Laden?

57. Who was president when the Soviet Union collapsed?

58. Who was president when America's territory grew by more than one-third extending out west, which caused a major fight between the northern and southern states over slavery?

59. Which president presided over meetings at Camp David with Egypt's president and Israel's prime minister? The result of these meetings ended the state of war between the two nations for which this president was awarded the Nobel Peace Prize.

60. Which president appointed Frederick Douglas ambassador to Haiti?

61. Who was president when Texas became the 28th state?

62. Who was president at the time of the construction of the first railroad?

63. Which president drastically reduced unemployment from 25% - 2%?

64. Which president recognized the state of Israel when it declared itself a nation?

65. Who was president when the new treaty the Gadsden Purchase was signed?

66. Which president signed the Civil Rights Act of 1870 & 1875 which guaranteed equal rights for African-Americans?

67. Which president was responsible for the improved performance of the postal service?

68. Who was president when the Treaty of Ghent was signed by British and American representatives ending the War of 1812?

69. Which president sponsored and signed the Civil Rights Bill of 1957, which was the first Civil Rights Bill since Reconstruction?

70. Which president signed Jay's Treaty with Great Britain?

71. Which president established the Department of Homeland Security?

72. As a conservationist, which president preserved approximately two hundred million acres for wildlife refugees, national forests, and reserves – which was five times the amount of land all his predecessors combined preserved?

73. Which president passed the Presidential Succession Act?

74. Which president signed California as a free state?

75. Which president fought against the Ku Klux Klan?

76. Which president vetoed the Second Bank of the United States?

77. Which president signed peace treaties with Germany and Austria after WWI?

78. Which president led the U.S. From isolationism to a victory over Nazi Germany and their allies during WWII?

79. Which president negotiated the Nuclear Test – Ban treaty?

80. Which president brought home the P.O.W.'s from Vietnam?

81. During his presidency a Civil Rights Act was passed recognizing African-Americans as citizens. Who was he?

82. Which president used atomic bombs on Hiroshima and

Nagasaki forcing Japan to surrender?

83. Which president established the Family and Medical Leave Act?

84. Which president signed the Americans with Disabilities Act?

85. Which president ended the draft?

86. Which president was responsible for nuclear weapons cuts?

87. Which president expanded the American boundaries to the Pacific Ocean?

88. Which president created the interstate highway system?

89. Which president made Hawaii a U.S. territory?

90. Which president set the standard for the office of the president?

91. Which president signed the Indian Citizenship Act? This granted citizenship to Native Americans and allowed them to

retain tribal land rights.

Answers

Chapter 9

1. Ronald Reagan

2. Abraham Lincoln

3. Andrew Johnson

*It is considered his most important foreign policy action.

4. Bill Clinton

5. Woodrow Wilson

6. Barack Obama

7. Thomas Jefferson

8. Woodrow Wilson

*Woodrow Wilson proclaimed the first national Mother's day as a day for Americans to fly the flag in honor of mothers whose son or sons had died in war.

9. Richard Nixon

10. Jimmy Carter

11. Bill Clinton

12. Chester Arthur

13. Barack Obama

14. Gerald Ford

15. Warren Harding

16. Richard Nixon

17. Ulysses S. Grant

18. Abraham Lincoln

19. Theodore Roosevelt

20. Lyndon B. Johnson

21. Bill Clinton

22. James Garfield

23. Dwight D. Eisenhower

24. James Madison

25. Theodore Roosevelt

26. Lyndon B. Johnson

27. Woodrow Wilson

28. John F. Kennedy

29. Richard Nixon

30. George W. Bush

31. Barack Obama

32. Thomas Jefferson

33. James Monroe

34. Richard Nixon

35. Harry Truman

36. Ronald Reagan

37. James Polk

*He acquired California from Mexico, settled the Oregon dispute, lowered tariffs, established a sub-treasury, and accomplished it all in one term and then retired from office.

38. William Harrison

39. John F. Kennedy

40. James Monroe

41. Gerald Ford

42. George H.W. Bush

43. John Adams

44. Thomas Jefferson

45. Dwight D. Eisenhower

46. Herbert Hoover

47. James Polk

*This added full control of what is the current states of Washington, Oregon, Idaho, and a portion of what is now the states of Montana and Wyoming.

48. John F. Kennedy

49. Rutherford B. Hayes

50. Richard Nixon

51. William McKinley

52. Gerald Ford

53. Thomas Jefferson

54. Dwight D. Eisenhower

55. Franklin D. Roosevelt

56. Barack Obama

57. George H.W. Bush

58. James Polk

59. Jimmy Carter

60. Benjamin Harrison

61. John Tyler

62. John Quincy Adams

63. Franklin D. Roosevelt

64. Harry Truman

65. Franklin Pierce

66. Ulysses S. Grant

67. William Taft

68. James Madison

*The Peace Treaty of Ghent ended the War of 1812.

69. Dwight D. Eisenhower

70. George Washington

71. George W. Bush

72. Theodore Roosevelt

73. Grover Cleveland

*In the case that a president died while in office this Act established the line of succession.

74. Millard Fillmore

75. Ulysses S. Grant

76. Andrew Jackson

77. Warren Harding

78. Franklin D. Roosevelt

79. John F. Kennedy

80. Richard Nixon

81. Andrew Johnson

82. Harry Truman

83. Bill Clinton

84. George H.W. Bush

85. Richard Nixon

86. Ronald Reagan

87. James Polk

88. Dwight D. Eisenhower

89. William McKinley

90. George Washington

91. Calvin Coolidge

10

Failures

1. Who was president during the "space race" with the Russians which cost American taxpayers $50 billion?

2. Which president's medical reform was to ensure "*everyone*" was insured; but not only did that not happen, but this insurance plan came at too high an expense for taxpayers?

3. Which president got us into the Vietnam War, which president escalated it, and which president got us out of the war?

4. Which president failed to defuse the Cold War?

5. Which president's policy of communist containment is what started the Cold War?

6. He fought for gun control, but his legislation requiring background checks on all guns purchased and a ban on assault weapons wasn't approved through Congress. Who was he?

7. Who was president when the XYZ Affair occurred, that led to an undeclared war called the Quasi-War?

8. Which president failed to heal the nation after the Civil War?

9. The Depression worsened during which president's administration?

10. The Alien and Sedition Acts were four bills that were signed into law that gave the power to deport foreigners as well as making it harder for new immigrants to vote. Which president signed these acts into law?

11. The White House knew about the plans for Rwandan genocide and did nothing to stop it. Who was president at the time?

12. Which president vetoed every equal rights bill that would help African-Americans?

13. This president justified the War of Iraq by claiming they had weapons of mass destruction. Who was he?

14. Racial divisions worsened during his presidency, instead of healing like people expected. Who was he?

15. Which president helped establish the League of Nations, and then failed to join the U.S. as a part?

16. Which president signed the Payne-Aldrich Bill which split up the Republican Party?

17. Which president failed to free the American hostages in Iran? A failed rescue attempt led his reputation to be inept and ineffective. Who was he?

18. Who was president when Prohibition, the banning of manufacture, sale, and transporting of alcohol went into effect? This president vetoed the National Prohibition Act, but his veto was overridden by Congress.

19. Sex scandals, including but not limited to the actress Marilyn Monroe, left this president with a bad reputation as a womanizer? Who was he?

20. Which president ended the Persian Gulf War without deposing Iraq's dictator, Saddam Hussein?

21. Who was president when the War of 1812 occurred? Some considered this war a second war for independence, however the United States suffered many costly defeats including the capture and burning of the nation's capital which included the Executive Mansion or White House.

22. Who was president when the housing market crashed, and it was the beginning of the recession?

23. Which president's stimulus did little to stimulate the economy?

24. Who was president during the rise of McCarthyism?

25. Which president failed to turn over documents subpoenaed by Congressional committees and claimed immunity from civil lawsuits claiming presidential immunity?

26. Which president was responsible for the passing of the Sherman Silver Purchase Act which depleted the gold supply?

27. Who was president during the hostage crisis in Iran?

28. Which president's 'War On Poverty' had no clear plan on how to go about fixing the problem?

29. Who was president during "The Plame Leak" which identified a covert operative in the CIA?

30. In June of 1950, the Korean War began when soldiers from the North Korean People's Army crossed the 38th parallel, the boundary between Soviet backed Democratic People's Republic of Korea to the north and pro-Western Republic of Korea to the south. This invasion was the first military action of the Cold War. America came to the defense of South Korea considering this a war against communism. What president ordered our troops into action to join in to aid South Korea as a "police action"? The fighting ended in July of 1953 when an armistice was signed, however no peace treaty was ever signed and the two Koreas are, technically at least, still at war.

31. Which president, and his administration, was involved with the cover up of their involvement of the scandal of Watergate?

32. Who was president when the 'The Brownsville Incident' occurred, whose action to the incident has remained a matter of controversy and an embarrassment to the army?

33. Which president is associated with 'The Monica Lewinsky Scandal'?

34. Which president relocated Japanese-Americans into internment camps?

35. The 'Teapot Dome Scandal' occurred during which president's administration?

36. Which president failed to defuse the Cold War and it became even more of a threat at the time he left the presidency than when he began it eight years earlier?

37. Which president gave up on his fight against slavery, deciding to fight only battles he could win?

38. What president was left as a lame duck his final two years in office due to failures in his administration?

39. What president's economic decisions were a contributing factor to the Panic of 1837?

40. Which president's administration failed at one of it's main objectives which was energy? This president believed it imperative that the U.S. not rely on foreign oil. The result with his fight against foreign oil was long lines at the gas stations and driving up oil prices. Who was he?

41. Which president tried unsuccessfully to have the words 'In God We Trust' removed from coins because he thought it was unconstitutional and sacrilegious?

42. Who was president during the Iran-Contra Affair?

43. Inconsistent on social issues, what president opposed discrimination against Chinese immigrants, but failed to support womens right to vote, equality for African-American voting rights, or the rights of American Indians to preserve their culture?

44. What president promised to ask Great Britain to give Ireland their independence, but failed to do so?

45. Which president turned Lincoln's historic bedroom into a means of receiving large donations or basically rented out Lincoln's room for the right price?

46. Which president was exposed concerning his enhanced interrogation techniques and prisoner abuse scandals?

47. Which president's Embargo Act, which restricted trade, ended up hurting Americans more than Britain or France who it was originally intended to hurt?

48. Which president failed to deal with the issue of slavery, instead leaving the matter for the states and territories to decide for themselves?

49. Which two presidents appointed positions of power to friends, family, and those who contributed to his campaign whether they were qualified or not?

50. Which president seems to hold the public's opinion as the worst president and most remembered for his sex scandals?

51. Who was president during the Bay of Pigs Invasion?

52. The Depression didn't end until the start of WWII. Who was president during the time of the Great Depression?

53. Who was president when the number of people having to turn to food stamps was at a record high?

54. Which president fired over one thousand postmasters in the South who weren't sympathetic to his policies? He fired so many that the Tenure of Office Act was passed prohibiting the president from firing any confirmed appointees without having the Senate's approval.

55. Which president received illegal campaign contributions by Indonesians which was called 'Indogate', which gave the impression American foreign policy was up for sale?

Answers

Chapter 10

1. John F. Kennedy

2. Barack Obama

3. John F. Kennedy got us into the war, Lyndon B. Johnson escalated it, and Nixon got us out of the war.

4. Dwight D. Eisenhower

5. Harry Truman

6. Barack Obama

7. John Adams

8. Andrew Johnson

9. Herbert Hoover

10. John Adams

11. Bill Clinton

12. Andrew Johnson

13. George W. Bush

14. Barack Obama

15. Woodrow Wilson

16. William Taft

17. Jimmy Carter

18. Woodrow Wilson

19. John F. Kennedy

20. George H.W. Bush

21. James Madison

22. George W. Bush

23. Barack Obama

24. Harry Truman

25. Bill Clinton

26. Benjamin Harrison

27. Jimmy Carter

28. Lyndon B. Johnson

29. George W. Bush

30. Harry Truman

31. Richard Nixon

32. Theodore Roosevelt

33. Bill Clinton

34. Franklin D. Roosevelt

35. Warren Harding

36. Dwight D. Eisenhower

37. Thomas Jefferson

38. George W. Bush

39. Andrew Jackson

40. Jimmy Carter

41. Theodore Roosevelt

42. Ronald Reagan

43. Grover Cleveland

44. Woodrow Wilson

45. Bill Clinton

46. George W. Bush

47. Thomas Jefferson

48. James Buchanan

49. Ulysses Grant and Warren Harding

50. Warren Harding

*He is not the only president that will be remembered for his sex scandals. Franklin Roosevelt, John F. Kennedy, and Bill Clinton have left the same legacy.

51. John F. Kennedy

52. Franklin Roosevelt

53. Barack Obama

54. Andrew Johnson

55. Bill Clinton

11

Works

Answers are given at the end of the chapter.

1. Which president signed legislation establishing Yellowstone National Park, the nation's first national park?

2. Which president announced a plan to develop and build space based weapons to protect American soil against Soviet nuclear missiles?

3. What was President Washington's last official act as president?

4. What president supported the Lewis and Clark Expedition?

5. What president gained popularity when he stood up to Khrushchev who people considered a Soviet bully?

6. Which president, in his State of the Union Address, spoke about being out of the recession; which many Americans didn't agree with due to the fact the number of families on food stamps, unemployed, and still struggling with the economic times?

7. Which president was in favor of civil rights? He appointed African-Americans to government positions and refused to appoint members of the Klu Klux Klan to office.

8. Which president's administration established several peace treaties with Native American tribes and approved a bill for the nation's new capital to be in a district along the Potomac River?

9. What president created the Federal Reserve?

10. What president vetoed the most bills?

11. During the administration of what president was the Department of Homeland Security established?

12. The Smithsonian Institute was established during his presidency. Who is he?

13. What president established these two new agencies during his administration: Department of Natural Resources and

Environmental Protection Agency?

14. On his last day in office what president signed a bill making Florida the 27th state?

15. What president was the driving force between the alliance between the U.S., Great Britain, and the Soviet Union which brought about the United Nations?

16. Which president awarded Rosa Parks the Presidential Medal of Freedom?

17. During whose presidency did his Secretary of State, William Seward, negotiate with Russia for the purchase of Alaska?

18. Same sex marriage was passed during what president's administration?

19. What president launched the Space Race?

20. What president signed into law a bill recognizing squatter's rights to occupy public lands?

21. Which president was instrumental in securing passage of the

religious freedom stature?

22. Who was president when Florida was purchased from Spain?

23. What president introduced the program Medicare?

24. What president was against the Chinese Exclusion Act which sought to close the U.S. border to Chinese immigrants?

25. What president took up the cause of the Clean Power Plan which was aimed at reducing greenhouse gas emissions, which he considered an important move against climate change?

26. Which president's foreign policy allowed the U.S. to have an active role in world affairs?

27. Which president encouraged creation of the first permanent White House library?

28. Who was president during the lowest unemployment rate in modern times?

29. Which president worked at alleviating poverty and creating a 'Great Society' for all Americans?

30. One of this president's main objectives was to focus on Reconstruction. Who was he?

31. Which president grew up in a wealthy family and lived a life of privilege, yet in his political life he worked hard to help the common man? His headmaster at school had instilled in him to help the less fortunate, and that lesson stayed with him when he could do the most towards this goal.

32. What president was known as a great humanitarian?

33. What president appointed Sandra Day O'Connor as the first woman in the U.S. Supreme Court?

34. What president fought hard against special favors to any economic groups? He stated the reason for this was that, "Federal Aid encourages the expectation of paternal care on the part of the government and weakens the sturdiness of our national character"?

35. In the year 1791, what president signed a bill authorizing Congress to tax alcohol?

36. What president during his administration took part in 'targeted killing' with unmanned drones?

37. Who was president when the Erie Canal was completed?

38. What president set the precedent for a limit of two terms as president?

39. What president fought to have the Panama Canal built?

40. What president called for an Indian Removal Act in his State of the Union message and signed the act into law?

41. What president appointed more women to federal posts than any other president?

42. Which president championed the cause for space exploration?

43. Which president declared war on global terrorism?

44. Who was president at the time Congress overrode a president on a bill that the president had vetoed?

45. What president blocked the annexation of Texas because he feared it might bring about a war with Mexico, and it also would add to slave territory?

Answers

Chapter 11

1. Ulysses S. Grant

2. Ronald Reagan

3. His last official act as president was to pardon the participants of the Whiskey Rebellion.

4. Thomas Jefferson

5. Richard Nixon

6. Barack Obama

7. Calvin Coolidge

8. George Washington

9. Woodrow Wilson

10. Grover Cleveland

11. George W. Bush

12. James Polk

13. Richard Nixon

14. John Tyler

15. Franklin D. Roosevelt

16. Bill Clinton

17. Andrew Johnson

*Alaska was purchased from Russia for $7 million. At the time critics called it 'Seward's Folly' thinking the purchase was a mistake.

18. Barack Obama

19. Dwight D. Eisenhower

20. John Tyler

*People who settled on and improved unsurveyed public land were entitled to first purchase rights.

21. James Madison

22. James Monroe

23. Lyndon B. Johnson

24. Benjamin Harrison

25. Barack Obama

26. William McKinley

27. Millard Fillmore

28. Bill Clinton

29. Lyndon B. Johnson

30. Ulysses S. Grant

31. Franklin D. Roosevelt

32. Herbert Hoover

33. Ronald Reagan

34. Grover Cleveland

35. George Washington

*Many people were not happy with this presidential act and they protested. This became known as The Whiskey Rebellion.

36. Barack Obama

37. John Quincy Adams

38. George Washington

39. Theodore Roosevelt

40. Andrew Jackson

41. Franklin D. Roosevelt

42. Lyndon B. Johnson

43. George W. Bush

44. Andrew Johnson

45. Martin Van Buren

12

Bad Boys / Busted

Answers are given at the end of the chapter.

1. Which president had extramarital affairs and left behind love letters to a mistress (the letters were written before he became president)?

2. Which president's vice president had to resign due to criminal charges, and then the president himself also had to resign at a later date?

3. In college this president was only an average student and once even slipped out the window of a classroom to get out of attending a lecture. Who was he?

4. The scandal of the Monica Lewinsky affair was at first denied by this president. This president was impeached for perjury and obstruction of justice, but remained in office. Who was he?

5. Which president, in a poker game, lost a set of White House china dating from the days of Benjamin Harrison?

6. Which president sent his mistress a ticket to his inauguration?

7. Which president was stopped for speeding and had to pay a $20 fine? Hint: He was on horseback.

8. Which president had several mistresses, even leaving one of them half of his $3 million estate?

9. Which president drank alcohol in the White House, which at that time was a violation of the Eighteenth Amendment?

10. Which president's reputation and respect suffered due to his ties with members of organized crime and his womanizing ways?

11. Which president was known to have romantic trysts with his mistress in the closet in the presidential office?

12. Which president's reputation suffered after his death when the Teapot Dome Scandal was uncovered, even though he himself wasn't involved in any illegal doings?

13. Which president had an affair with his wife's social secretary?

14. How many presidents had illegitimate children?

15. Which of our presidents left office in disgrace over the Watergate Scandal?

16. How many U.S. presidents are known to have smoked marijuana?

17. Which president was married to a woman who was already married to another man?

18. Presidents have been known to lie to the American public. Some of the presidents' lies have been forgiven more readily than others. Can you name a few of the presidents and the lies that have gone down in history with them?

19. Which president was involved in the Star Route Scandal, a scheme where postal officials received bribes in exchange for giving postal delivery contracts to southern areas?

20. Which president's administration was involved in the Benghazi cover up?

Answers

Chapter 12

1. Warren Harding

2. Richard Nixon

3. Franklin D. Roosevelt

4. Bill Clinton

*It later came out that Monica Lewinsky wasn't the only one that pointed the finger at him about his sexual activities.

5. Warren Harding

6. Franklin D. Roosevelt

7. Ulysses S. Grant

8. Franklin D. Roosevelt

9. Warren Harding

10. John F. Kennedy

11. Warren Harding

12. Warren Harding

13. Franklin D. Roosevelt

*When his wife discovered the affair she gave him an ultimatum –
stop seeing the other woman or she would divorce him. He agreed
to stop seeing the woman, but continued seeing her for the rest of
his life. She was even by his side when he died.

14. 5

*Thomas Jefferson had illegitimate children with his slave. He
was the father of one, if not all six, of her children.

William H. Harrison also had children with one of his slaves.

John Tyler also was rumored to have at least one child with a
slave, but has not been proven one way or the other.

Grover Cleveland. There are two stories about this: One is that the mother of his illegitimate child threatened to go to the authorities due to Grover raping her which resulted in the child. He threatened her life and had her placed in a mental asylum, where she was later let go after it was determined she wasn't crazy, but instead had a president out to destroy her to cover up his own actions. The other story was she was a mistress that he had a consensual affair with and the child was a result of this affair. He did have her committed to a mental asylum where she was soon released when it was found that she had no mental health problems. The child was given up for adoption.

Warren Harding had an illegitimate child with a mistress.

Only Thomas Jefferson's and Warren Harding's illegitimate children have been proven through DNA testing. The other presidents are rumors that have not been substantiated.

15. Richard Nixon

16. Eleven. There could have been more as many farmers grew hemp back in the early days of the U.S.

The presidents known to have smoked are:

George Washington – He made notes in his diary about growing hemp and about it's use for smoking.

Thomas Jefferson

James Madison

James Monroe – He smoked hashish up until his death.

Andrew Jackson – He was known to have smoked with his troops.

Zachary Taylor - He was known to have smoked with his troops.

Franklin Pierce - He was known to have smoked with his troops during the Mexican-American War.

John F. Kennedy – He smoked using his back pain as the reason and once after smoking a few joints stated, "Suppose the Russians did something now."

Bill Clinton – He said he didn't inhale, but a college mate of his said he didn't have to inhale, he loved his pot brownies.

George W. Bush – He wouldn't admit to it when asked by a reporter, as he said he didn't want young children to follow in his footsteps.

Barack Obama

17. Andrew Jackson

*You can't really blame him, though some people were in an uproar about it, as both him and his wife were under the impression the divorce had been finalized before they were married.

18. If you remember one or two of these that's great. You may remember more as you read below. It appears that they forget that everything they say is on film and someone, somewhere is going to bring it up and expose them.

Listed below are some of the lies that the public didn't forget.

Andrew Jackson lied in his campaign stating he stood for one thing and proved differently when he was actually elected.

James Polk lied to Congress saying Mexico had invaded the U.S. which led to the Mexican-American War.

Abraham Lincoln lied about his views on slavery.

William McKinley lied about Spain blowing up a U.S. warship in Cuba with no evidence whatsoever to back up his statement. This lie led to the Spanish-American War.

Franklin D. Roosevelt – He told America, "Your boys are not going to be sent into any foreign wars." He also lied to different men telling them he wanted them for his vice-president when he had no intention on choosing any of them.

Dwight D. Eisenhower lied about the U.S. flying spy planes over the Soviet Union, but the truth came out when one of the planes was shot down and the pilot was captured

John F. Kennedy – He reassured America that the U.S. wasn't planning any military intervention in Cuba, while at the same time planning an invasion.

Lyndon B. Johnson lied about the cost of the Vietnam War not only to the American people but to Congress.

Nixon lied about his knowledge or of having any part of Watergate. His lies didn't save him as he later resigned over this issue.

Ronald Reagan firmly stated that America didn't trade weapons or anything else to Iran for hostages.

George H.W. Bush told America to read his lips that he wasn't going to raise taxes.

Bill Clinton told the American public that he did not have sex with that woman. Later, he had a word war on the definition of the word 'is' and danced around the issue instead of owning up to his misbehavior.

George W Bush convinced Americans Iraq had weapons of mass destruction and because of that lie he had the backing of the people for going to war with Iraq. When it was discovered that he hadn't been truthful about the matter it cost him his reputation and will leave a black mark on his legacy as president.

Barack Obama – With Obamacare he reassured the American public if they already had insurance and were happy with it they could keep it.

19. James Garfield

20. Barack Obama

13

Middle Names of the Presidents

Answers are given at the end of the chapter.

Match the middle names to the correct president

1. Baines

2. Calvin

3. Alan

4. Fitzgerald

5. Abram

6. Milhous

7. Howard

8. Herbert Walker

9. S (for Shippe or Solomon)

*His parents only gave him the initial S for his middle name which was to honor both his grandfathers.

10. Hussein

11. Knox

12. Quincy

13. Woodrow

14. Birchard

15. Walker

16. Simpson

17. Rudolph

18. Grover

19. Delano

20. Gamaliel

21. David

22. Jefferson

23. Clark

24. Henry

25. Earl

26. Wilson

Answers

Chapter 13

1. Lyndon B. Johnson

2. Calvin Coolidge

3. Chester Arthur

4. John F. Kennedy

5. James Garfield

6. Richard Nixon

7. Howard Taft

8. George H.W. Bush

9. Harry Truman

10. Barack Obama

11. James Polk

12. John Quincy Adams

13. Woodrow Wilson

14. Rutherford B. Hayes

15. George W. Bush

16. Ulysses S. Grant

17. Gerald Ford

18. Grover Cleveland

19. Franklin D. Roosevelt

20. Warren Harding

21. Dwight D. Eisenhower

22. Bill Clinton

23. Herbert Hoover

24. William Henry Harrison

25. Jimmy Carter

26. Ronald Reagan

14

Nicknames

Answers are given at the end of the chapter.

1. What does POTUS stand for?

2. The Secret Service has a code name for the president for security reasons. Which president was given the code name Lance?

3. What president was given the code name Rawhide by the Secret Service?

4. Which president was nicknamed Old Hickory because of his toughness?

5. Which president was sometimes called Jack by his family and friends?

6. Which president, while in school, was nicknamed Big Lub due to his size?

7. Which president is sometimes referred to as Slick Willie?

8. Which president had the nickname The Little Magician due to his reputation as a crafty partisan?

9. Which president is sometimes referred to as Father of the Constitution?

10. Which president had the nickname Dutch?

11. Which president was called the Gentleman Boss?

12. Which president was called His Rotundity?

13. Which president was given the nickname of Little Ben?

14. Which president was called Old Man Eloquent?

15. Which president had the nickname Ten-Cent Jimmy?

16. Which president was nicknamed Unconditional Surrender?

17. Which president was nicknamed Tricky Dick?

18. Which president was called 'Father of His Country' and 'Father of The Country'?

19. Which president was called His Fraudulency?

20. What president was known as Silent Cal?

21. Which president had earned the nickname Old Rough and Ready?

22. Which president's nickname was Old Kinderhook?

23. What president was also nicknamed The Gipper?

24. Which president had the nickname Old Tippecanoe?

25. What president was referred to as the Rail Splitter?

26. Which president was sometimes referred to as the Peanut Farmer?

27. Which president was called Mr. Nice Guy?

28. Which president was sometimes called by his initials FDR?

29. Which president was sometimes called by his initials LBJ?

30. Which president was sometimes called by his initials JFK?

31. Which president was called His Accidency, but probably not to his face?

32. Which president was known as Ike?

33. Which president was called Teddy?

Answers

Chapter 14

1. President of the United States

2. John F. Kennedy

3. Ronald Reagan

4. Andrew Jackson

5. John F. Kennedy

6. William Howard Taft

7. Bill Clinton

8. Martin Van Buren

9. James Madison

10. Ronald Reagan

*This was his father's nickname for him.

11. Chester Arthur

12. John Adams

13. Benjamin Harrison

14. John Quincy Adams

15. James Buchanan

*He was given this name when he said ten cents was fair pay for a day's manual labor.

16. Ulysses S. Grant

17. Richard Nixon

18. George Washington

19. Rutherford B. Hayes

*Due to the disputed results of the election many Democrats didn't consider him to be the legitimate president.

20. Calvin Coolidge

21. Zachary Taylor

22. Martin Van Buren

23. Ronald Reagan

24. William H. Harrison

*This nickname was in reference to Harrison's victory at the Battle of Tippecanoe.

25. Abraham Lincoln

26. Jimmy Carter

27. Gerald Ford

28. Franklin D. Roosevelt

29. Lyndon B. Johnson

30. John F. Kennedy

31. John Tyler

32. Dwight D. Eisenhower

33. Theodore Roosevelt

15

War

Answers are given at the end of the chapter.

Many presidents fought in wars prior to becoming president. Do you know who these future presidents are?

1. How many future presidents fought in the Revolutionary War?

2. Which president was famous for the Battle of Tippecanoe?

3. Which president, when just a young boy, watched the Battle of Bunker Hill that was fought near his family farm?

4. What future president was a part of the Rough Riders during the Spanish-American War?

5. Who was president when the U.S. invaded Panama and overthrew the dictator Noriega?

6. Which future president fought against Indians on the U.S. frontier?

7. During the Mexican War, what future president barely escaped injury as a shot tore through his sleeve and another passed through the front of his coat taking off a button?

8. Which president was responsible for ending the Korean War?

9. Which president was responsible for U.S. invading Iraq after convincing the American public that Iraq was in possession of weapons of mass destruction?

10. Which president was responsible for the use of the atomic bomb against Japan to put an end to WWII?

11. Who was the last Civil War general to become president?

12. Which president had served in the army for four decades which included the War of 1812, Black Hawk War, and the second Seminole Wars?

13. In the War of 1812, which future president became a hero when he defeated the British at New Orleans?

14. Which future president had opposed the use of the atomic bomb against Japan?

15. When this president took office, the war in Vietnam was costing Americans $60 – $80 million dollars a day and were losing the lives of approximately three hundred American soldiers a week. This president's main concern when he took office was to solve this issue. Who was he?

16. Which future president led the invasion known in history as D-Day?

17. Confederate General Robert E. Lee surrendered to this future president at Appomattox Court House in Virginia putting an end to the Civil War. Who was he?

18. Which president stated detainees of terrorists were not protected by the Geneva Convention, and as a result many of the detainees were tortured?

19. What future president commanded the Union Army during the Civil War?

20. Who was president during the Mexican-American War?

21. During the Civil War what future president was the only Southern senator to remain loyal to the Union?

22. Which president won a Nobel Peace Prize for mediating the Russo-Japanese War?

23. The Treaty of Versailles, which brought an end to WWI, was drafted by the Big Four powers – those of the United States, Great Britain, France, and Italy. What U.S. president helped draft this treaty?

23. What president received the Distinguished Flying Cross for bravery?

25. The Spanish-American War was declared while he was president. Who was he?

26. What future president survived four plane crashes during WWII?

27. Who was president immediately prior to the Civil War?

28. Who was president when the United States invaded Afghanistan to overthrow the Taliban government?

29. Which president led the U.S. into the Korean War?

30. What future president, on Christmas night in the year 1776, led his men across the Delaware River and attacked the Hessian mercenaries?

31. Which president led the nation into war with Spain over Cuban independence?

32. A few weeks after he left the office of the presidency, Confederates fired on Ft. Sumter which was the beginning of the Civil War. Who was the president who had just left office?

33. What future president was in the Navy and in a torpedo boat when it was rammed by a Japanese warship? This future president led the survivors to a nearby island where they were later rescued.

34. Who was president when British troops set fire to the White House and the Capitol?

35. Which future president was with George Washington and his troops at Valley Forge during the harsh winter of 1777 – 1778?

36. Which future president sent troops to China to help put an end to the Boxer Rebellion, an uprising against foreign intervention in China?

37. During WWII this future president's plane was hit and on fire, but he continued on and successfully bombed his target before ejecting out of his plane. He was rescued in the water by an American submarine. Who was he?

38. Which future president was appointed Commander-in-Chief of the Colonial forces against Great Britain?

39. Which president was a general and a hero in the Mexican-American War and the War of 1812?

40. At the beginning of WWI what president declared America neutral, but by 1917 he asked Congress to declare war when Germany sunk American ships and ignored U.S. neutrality? Who was he?

41. What future president fought in the Revolutionary War when he was a teenager?

42. During the War of 1812, which president's wife remained at the Executive Mansion as British troops advanced into Washington, D.C. so she could see to the safe removal of national treasures?

Who was president at this time?

43. Who was president at the end of WWII?

44. What president led the U.S. through WWI?

45. The day after Pearl Harbor was bombed by the Japanese, which president declared war on Japan?

46. What future president had winter quarters in the year 1777 at Valley Forge during the Revolutionary War?

47. What president was a pilot in the National Guard?

48. Who was president during the war with the Seminole Indians in Florida?

49. Which president declared war which was known as Operation Desert Storm or the Persian Gulf War?

50. What future president served as a military aide to General Douglas MacArthur?

51. Who was the only president who had been a prisoner of war?

52. In 1863, what president reshaped the cause of the war from keeping the union intact to abolishing slavery?

53. What president organized a coalition with other countries in an assault against Iraq after they invaded Kuwait?

54. Which future president enlisted in the Black Hawk War and seeing no action, after leaving the military made the joke that the only blood he lost in the war was to mosquitoes?

55. Which president created an air lift to get supplies to the people of Berlin when the Russians blockaded western areas of Berlin?

56. Which future president was taken prisoner by British soldiers when they invaded the Carolinas? While prisoner he refused to shine an officer's boots, the officer then hit this future president across the face with his saber leaving a scar. Who was he?

57. Who was president during the days when the world was on the brink of nuclear annihilation known as the Cuban Missile Crisis?

58. What future president was wounded during the American Revolutionary War?

59. What future president was the sole supporter of his family during the Civil War, and because of this was able to pay a substitute to take his place in the war?

60. Can you name the eight presidents with the most 'impressive' military record that fought for our country? (They aren't the only ones, just the ones with the most impressive records.)

61. Can you name the four presidents who fought or served in the Revolutionary War?

62. Can you name the four presidents who fought or served in the War of 1812?

63. Can you name the two presidents who fought or served in the Black Hawk War?

64. Can you name the three presidents that fought or served in the Mexican-American War?

65. Can you name the eight presidents who fought or served in the Civil War?

66. Can you name the president who fought in the Spanish-American War?

67. Can you name the two presidents who fought or served in WWI?

68. Can you name the seven presidents who fought or served in WWII?

69. Can you name the president who fought or served in the Korean War?

70. Can you name the president who fought in the Vietnam War?

Answers

Chapter 15

1. Four

2. William H. Harrison

3. John Quincy Adams

4. Theodore Roosevelt

5. George H.W. Bush

6. William H. Harrison

7. Zachary Taylor

8. Dwight D. Eisenhower

9. George W. Bush

10. Harry Truman

11. Benjamin Harrison

12. Zachary Taylor

13. Andrew Jackson

14. Dwight D. Eisenhower

15. Richard Nixon

16. Dwight D. Eisenhower

17. Ulysses S. Grant

18. George W. Bush

19. Ulysses S. Grant

20. James Polk

21. Andrew Johnson

22. Theodore Roosevelt

23. Woodrow Wilson

24. George H.W. Bush

25. William McKinley

26. George H.W. Bush

27. James Buchanan

28. George W. Bush

29. Harry Truman

30. George Washington

31. William McKinley

*The end result was U.S. possession over Puerto Rico, Guam, and the Philippines.

32. James Buchanan

33. John F. Kennedy

34. James Madison

35. James Monroe

36. William McKinley

37. George H.W. Bush

38. George Washington

39. Zachary Taylor

40. Woodrow Wilson

41. James Monroe

42. James Madison

43. Harry Truman

44. Woodrow Wilson

45. Franklin D. Roosevelt

*President Roosevelt actually stated his reason on why we should declare war before a joint session of Congress, which then did declare war on Japan.

46. George Washington

47. George W. Bush

48. Martin Van Buren

49. George H.W. Bush

Bonus questions:

Our troops were headquartered in what country and to liberate what country?

Answers to bonus questions:

They were headquartered in Saudi Arabia to liberate Kuwait.

50. Dwight D. Eisenhower

51. Andrew Jackson

52. Abraham Lincoln

53. George H.W. Bush

54. Abraham Lincoln

55. Harry Truman

56. Andrew Jackson

57. John F. Kennedy

58. James Monroe

59. Grover Cleveland

60. George Washington, Andrew Jackson, Zachary Taylor, Ulysses S. Grant, Theodore Roosevelt, Dwight D. Eisenhower, John F. Kennedy, and George H.W. Bush

61. George Washington, James Madison, James Monroe, and Andrew Jackson

62. Andrew Jackson, William H. Harrison, John Tyler, and Zachary Taylor

63. Abraham Lincoln and Zachary Taylor

64. Zachary Taylor, Franklin Pierce, and Ulysses S. Grant

65. Andrew Johnson, Ulysses S. Grant, Rutherford B. Hayes, James Garfield, Chester Arthur, Benjamin Harrison, William McKinley, and Millard Fillmore

66. Theodore Roosevelt

67. Harry Truman and Dwight D. Eisenhower

68. Dwight D. Eisenhower, John F. Kennedy, Lyndon B. Johnson, Richard Nixon, Gerald Ford, Ronald Reagan, and George H.W. Bush

69. Jimmy Carter

70. George W. Bush

16

Vice-Presidents

Answers are given at the end of the chapter.

Match the vice-presidents to the president they served under.

1. Al Gore

2. Nelson Rockefeller

3. John Breckinridge

4. William King

5. Charles Dawes

6. George Clinton and Elbridge Gerry

7. Adlai Stevenson

8. John Adams

9. George Clinton

10. Joe Biden

11. Alben Barkley

12. Daniel Tompkins

13. Chester Arthur

14. Calvin Coolidge

15. George H.W. Bush

16. Hannibal Hamlin and Andrew Johnson

17. Charles Curtis

18. Garret Hobart and Theodore Roosevelt

19. Aaron Burr and George Clinton

20. Walter Mondale

21. William Wheeler

22. Schuyler Colfax and Henry Wilson

23. Richard Nixon

24. Dick Cheney

25. Spiro Agnew and Gerald Ford

26. There are four presidents that didn't have a vice president. Can you name them?

27. Thomas Hendricks

28. John Nance Garner, Henry Wallace, and Harry Truman

29. Dan Quayle

30. Millard Fillmore

31. Thomas Jefferson

32. Martin Van Buren

33. James Sherman

34. John Calhoun

35. Thomas Marshall

36. Charles Fairbanks

37. Levi Morton

38. Richard Johnson

39. John Tyler

40. George Dallas

41. Lyndon B. Johnson

42. Hubert Humphrey

43. Who was vice-president and while visiting his father in Vermont was notified of the president's death? He was sworn into office by his father, a notary public, at 2:47 A.M. On August 3, 1923, by the light of a kerosene lamp. Who is he?

44. Which vice president succeeded to the presidency when the acting president resigned?

45. Who was the first vice president to attend cabinet meetings and have official duties?

46. How many presidents served as vice-presidents before becoming presidents? Can you name them?

47. Which vice-president was the first appointed under provision of the Twenty-fifth Amendment?

48. Who is our current vice-president?

49. Other than Vice-President Agnew, who was the only other vice-president to resign? He did so in order to accept election to the Senate.

50. What is the purpose of the Twenty-fifth Amendment?

Answers

Chapter 16

1. Bill Clinton

2. Gerald Ford

3. James Buchanan

4. Franklin Pierce

5. Calvin Coolidge

6. James Madison (1813 – 1814)

7. Grover Cleveland's second term

8. George Washington

9. Thomas Jefferson (1805 – 1809)   OR/AND   James Madison (1809 – 1812)

10. Barack Obama

11. Harry Truman

12. James Monroe

13. James Garfield

14. Warren Harding

15. Ronald Reagan

16. Abraham Lincoln

17. Herbert Hoover

18. William McKinley

19. Thomas Jefferson

20. Jimmy Carter

21. Rutherford B. Hayes

22. Ulysses S. Grant

23. Dwight D. Eisenhower

24. George W. Bush

25. Richard Nixon

26. John Tyler, Millard Fillmore, Andrew Johnson, and Chester Arthur

27. Grover Cleveland during his first term of office.

28. Franklin D. Roosevelt

29. George H.W. Bush

30. Zachary Taylor

31. John Adams

32. Andrew Jackson

33. William Taft

34. John Quincy Adams (1825 – 1829)   AND/OR   Andrew Jackson (1829 – 1832)

35. Woodrow Wilson

36. Theodore Roosevelt

37. Benjamin Harrison

38. Martin Van Buren

39. William H. Harrison

40. James Polk

41. John F. Kennedy

42. Lyndon B. Johnson

43. Calvin Coolidge

44. Gerald Ford

45. Calvin Coolidge

46. 14 as of this date.

They are:

John Adams (elected)

Thomas Jefferson (elected)

Martin Van Buren (elected)

John Tyler (succeeded)

Millard Fillmore (succeeded)

Andrew Johnson (succeeded)

Chester Arthur (succeeded)

Theodore Roosevelt (succeeded)

Calvin Coolidge (succeeded)

Harry Truman (succeeded)

Richard Nixon (elected)

Lyndon B. Johnson (succeeded)

Gerald Ford (succeeded due to previous president's resignation)

George H.W. Bush (elected)

47. Gerald Ford. He became president when President Nixon resigned.

48. Answers will vary depending on date.

49. John Calhoun

50. The Twenty-fifth Amendment deals with the succession to the presidency and establishes the procedures for filling a vacancy of the vice-president; as well as responding to presidential disabilities.

17

First Ladies

Answers are given at the end of the chapter.

Match the First Ladies to their husbands, the President.

1. Grace Anna Goodhue

2. Julia Boggs Dent

3. Nancy Davis

4. Ida Saxton

5. Eliza McCardle

6. Helen Louise Herron, called "Nellie"

7. Elizabeth Virginia Wallace, called "Bess"

8. Barbara Pierce

9. Margaret Mackall Smith, called "Peggy"

10. Thelma Catherine, called "Pat"

11. Lucretia Rudolph

12. Elizabeth Ann Bloomer, called "Betty"

13. Anna Tuthill Symmes

14. Caroline Scott

15. Francis Folsom

16. Elizabeth Kurtright

17. Eleanor Rosalyn Smith, called "Rosalynn"

18. Ellen Louise Axson (first wife), Edith Bolling Galt (second wife)

19. Jacqueline Lee Bouvier, called "Jackie"

20. Abigail Smith

21. Mary Ann Todd

22. Rachel Donelson Robards

23. Mamie Geneva Doud, called "Mamie"

24. Even though this First Lady didn't live long enough to see her husband become president she is still considered a First Lady. Martha Wayles Skelton

25. Lucy Ware Webb

26. Anna Eleanor Roosevelt, called "Eleanor"

27. Louisa Catherine Johnson

28. Martha Dandridge Custis

29. Lou Henry

30. Jane Means Appleton

31. Laura Lane Welch

32. Edith Kermit Carow (She was the president's second wife and was the First Lady. His first wife died before he became president.)

33. Sarah Childress

34. Dolly Payne Todd

35. Claudia Alta Taylor, went by "Lady Bird"

36. Letitia Christian (first wife), Julia Gardiner (second wife)

37. Abigail Powers

38. Florence Mabel

39. Michelle LeVaughn Robinson

Answers

Chapter 17

1. Calvin Coolidge

2. Ulysses S. Grant

3. Ronald Reagan

4. William McKinley

5. Andrew Johnson

6. William H. Taft

7. Harry Truman

8. George H.W. Bush

9. Zachary Taylor

10. Richard Nixon

11. James Garfield

12. Gerald Ford

13. William H. Harrison

14. Benjamin Harrison

15. Grover Cleveland

16. James Monroe

17. Jimmy Carter

18. Woodrow Wilson

19. John F. Kennedy

20. John Adams

21. Abraham Lincoln

22. Andrew Jackson

23. Dwight D. Eisenhower

24. Thomas Jefferson

25. Rutherford B. Hayes

26. Franklin D. Roosevelt

27. John Quincy Adams

28. George Washington

29. Herbert Hoover

30. Franklin Pierce

31. George W. Bush

32. Theodore Roosevelt

33. James Polk

34. James Madison

35. Lyndon B. Johnson

36. John Tyler

37. Millard Fillmore

38. Warren Harding

39. Barack Obama

18

Fun Facts About The Presidents

Answers are given at the end of the chapter.

1. Which president was ambidextrous (could write with either hand)?

2. Which president was known for keeping a jar of jelly beans on his desk?

3. Which president was blind in one eye from a boxing match he was in?

4. Who is the only president in the twentieth century to not have a college degree?

5. Which president kept sheep on the White House lawn to crop

the grass during WWI because of the man power shortage?

6. During his college days, which president was Most Valuable Player and was offered a football career by the Green Bay Packers and the Detroit Lions?

7. Which president made a parachute jump on his 80th, 85th and 90th birthday?

8. True or False.

Did Ulysses S. Grant wear false teeth?

9. Which president stated he had seen a UFO?

10. Which president had blue marks on his legs all his life because he wore buckskin breeches and got caught in the rain and they shrank?

11. Which president had a photographic memory?

12. Which president first installed a billiard table in the White House?

13. Which president hated music of all types?

14. Which president, at the age of fifteen, ran away from home?

15. Which president was nauseated by the sight of animal blood?

16. Which president was in great shape, and even during his presidential days he walked over three miles a day and swam in the Potomac River?

17. What president could read about two thousand words a minute?

18. What president was captain of Yale University's baseball team?

19. What president had the first bathtub installed in the White House?

20. Which president is known to dislike broccoli and said, "I'm President of the United States, and I'm not going to eat any more broccoli"?

21. As a child, which president was too sickly to go to school?

22. Which president hired Louis Comfort Tiffany to redecorate the state rooms before moving into the White House?

23. What kind of school did Abraham Lincoln go to? Here's a hint: Everyone said their lessons out loud.

24. Which president was a speed reader and had been recorded reading up to two thousand words per minute?

25. Who is the only president to have been stuck in the White House bathtub?

26. Which president could read seven languages?

27. Which president was an accomplished pianist who played for a White House gathering when Kennedy was president?

28. Which president was an athlete and played baseball, football, rugby, and basketball?

29. Which president painted his golf balls black in the winter so he could see them in the snow?

30. Which president gave up horseback riding and instead took up

riding a mechanical horse?

31. Which president was an ordained minister?

32. Which president was good friends with the author Nathaniel Hawthorne? He was vacationing with Hawthorne when he died in his sleep.

33. Which president never voted until he was sixty two years of age?

34. Who is the only president to have been a professional actor?

35. At one time which president was an owner of the Texas Rangers baseball team?

36. Which future president had the job of scrubbing toilets while in the navy?

37. Which president had a putting green installed on the White House lawn because of his love of the game of golf?

38. Which president served hot dogs to King George VI of England and the queen when they paid a visit to his home?

39. Which president, while in college took part in football, track, captain of the swim team, drama, and was student council president?

40. Which president had to sleep in the hall at one time due to having so many visitors at the White House?

41. What president measured at 6'4"?

42. What president collected comic books?

43. Who was the only bachelor to be president in American history?

44. Which president was one of, if not "the most", accomplished athletes ever to become president?

45. Who was the only president to earn a doctorate?

46. What president played the saxophone?

47. Which president was the oldest being elected at the age of sixty nine?

48. What president loved to paint for relaxation? He couldn't draw, so someone else would sketch the picture and he would paint it.

49. Which president worked as a fashion model?

50. Which president enjoyed going to nightclubs (while president)?

51. Which president had a job as a Yellowstone Park Ranger?

52. Which president was the youngest president elected to office?

53. Who was president at the time that Charles Lindbergh made his historic flight across the Atlantic Ocean?

54. Which president initiated the custom of throwing the first ball at the beginning of baseball season?

55. Which president had an Airedale dog, named Laddie Boy, who delivered his newspapers and is now depicted in a statue in the Smithsonian?

56. Which president had a son that was an actor and played on a soap opera?

57. Which president was the youngest pilot in the Navy?

58. Which president was a skilled chef?

59. Which president had a large wardrobe which included eighty pairs of pants and often changed clothes several times a day?

60. Which president was a stamp collector and even made suggestions on designs of new commemorative stamps?

61. Which president smoked twenty cigars a day?

62. Which president was known to begin his day at 5:00 A.M. In order to practice the piano?

63. Which president, receiving his wings at the age of nineteen, was the nation's youngest commissioned pilot?

64. Which president was the teddy bear named after?

65. Who was president when the first telephone was installed in the White House?

66. Who was the only president to weigh under one hundred pounds?

67. Which president could read English, Latin, French, and Greek?

68. Which president was a mimic, and loved to tell dialect jokes in English, Irish, and Scottish accents?

69. Which president banned liquor from the White House?

70. Who was the tallest president?

71. Who was the shortest president?

Answers

Chapter 18

1. James Garfield

2. Ronald Reagan

3. Theodore Roosevelt

4. Harry Truman

5. Woodrow Wilson

6. Gerald Ford

7. George H.W. Bush

8. True

9. Jimmy Carter

10. Abraham Lincoln

11. Theodore Roosevelt

*He could read a page out of a book in the time it took most people to read a single sentence.

12. John Quincy Adams

13. Ulysses S. Grant

14. Lyndon B. Johnson

15. Ulysses S. Grant

*This was due to witnessing some of the bloodiest battles in history.

16. John Quincy Adams

17. John F. Kennedy

18. George H.W. Bush

19. Millard Fillmore

20. George H.W. Bush

21. Theodore Roosevelt

22. Chester Arthur

23. Blab school

24. Jimmy Carter, John F. Kennedy, and Theodore Roosevelt

25. William Taft

*He weighed between three hundred and three hundred fifty pounds while in office. After getting stuck in the bathtub he ordered a new tub, one that was large enough to hold four men.

26. John Adams

27. Harry Truman

28. George W. Bush

29. Woodrow Wilson

30. Calvin Coolidge

31. James Garfield

32. Franklin Pierce

33. Zachary Taylor

34. Ronald Reagan

*His first wife who he was divorced from was a well-known actress also.

35. George W. Bush

36. Jimmy Carter

37. Dwight D. Eisenhower

38. Franklin D. Roosevelt

39. Ronald Reagan

40. James Buchanan

*The Prince of Wales is the one who brought so many guests that the president had to sleep in the hall.

41. Abraham Lincoln

42. Barack Obama

43. James Buchanan

44. Gerald Ford

45. Woodrow Wilson

46. Bill Clinton

47. Ronald Reagan

48. Dwight D. Eisenhower

49. Gerald Ford

*During his days at Yale he had invested in a modeling agency. He posed for ski-wear ads.

50. Chester Arthur

51. Gerald Ford

52. John F. Kennedy

53. Calvin Coolidge

54. William Taft

55. Warren Harding

56. Gerald Ford

57. George H.W. Bush

58. Dwight D. Eisenhower

59. Chester Arthur

60. Franklin Roosevelt

61. Ulysses S. Grant

62. Harry Truman

63. George H.W. Bush

64. Theodore Roosevelt

*The teddy bear was named after him when a cartoon was put out showing Theodore Roosevelt saving the life of a bear cub while hunting.

65. Rutherford B. Hayes

66. James Madison

*He was 5'4 and weighed ninety-eight pounds.

67. Thomas Jefferson

68. Woodrow Wilson

69. Rutherford B. Hayes

70. Abraham Lincoln at 6'4".

71. James Madison at 5'4" and weighing in at just under one hundred pounds.

19

Lists

Answers are given at the end of the chapter.

1. Write a list naming the first ten presidents in order.

2. List the names of all the presidents. They don't have to be in order, but awesome if you can.

3. How many vice presidents later became president? Can you name them. They don't have to be in order.

4. Write a list giving the names of ten vice presidents.

5. Write a list naming the last ten presidents.

6. Can you name ten First Ladies?

7. How many presidents can you name along with the name of the First Lady they were married to?

8. Who do you think has been the best president, and why do you think so?

9. Who do you think has been our worst president, and why do you think so?

10. What do you think are important requirements or attributes you would look for, or expect to find, in a president you would choose to vote for?

11. List the requirements a candidate for President of the United States must meet before running for president?

12. Where are the requirements for the United States president's eligibility written?

13. How many presidents are still alive today? Who are they?

Answers

Chapter 19

1.

George Washington

John Adams

Thomas Jefferson

James Madison

James Monroe

John Quincy Adams

Andrew Jackson

Martin Van Buren

William Henry Harrison

John Tyler

2.

1. George Washington

2. John Adams

3. Thomas Jefferson

4. James Madison

5. James Monroe

6. John Quincy Adams

7. Andrew Jackson

8. Martin Van Buren

9. William H. Harrison

10. John Tyler

11. James Polk

12. Zachary Taylor

13. Millard Fillmore

14. Franklin Pierce

15. James Buchanan

16. Abraham Lincoln

17. Andrew Johnson

18. Ulysses S. Grant

19. Rutherford B. Hayes

20. James Garfield

21. Chester Arthur

22. Grover Cleveland

23. Benjamin Harrison

24. Grover Cleveland

25. William McKinley

26. Theodore Roosevelt

27. William Taft

28. Woodrow Wilson

29. Warren Harding

30. Calvin Coolidge

31. Herbert Hoover

32. Franklin D. Roosevelt

33. Harry Truman

34. Dwight D. Eisenhower

35. John F. Kennedy

36. Lyndon B. Johnson

37. Richard Nixon

38. Gerald Ford

39. Jimmy Carter

40. Ronald Reagan

41. George H.W. Bush

42. Bill Clinton

43. George W. Bush

44. Barack Obama

3. 14

John Adams

Thomas Jefferson

Martin Van Buren

John Tyler

Millard Fillmore

Andrew Johnson

Chester Arthur

Theodore Roosevelt

Calvin Coolidge

Harry Truman

Lyndon B. Johnson

Richard Nixon

Gerald Ford

George H.W. Bush

4. Any ten out of this list would be correct.

1. J. Adams

2. T. Jefferson

3. A. Burr / G. Clinton

4. G. Clinton / E. Gerry

5. D. Tompkins

6. J. Calhoun

7. J. Calhoun / M. Van Buren

8. R. Johnson

9. J. Tyler

10. -

11. G. Dallas

12. M. Fillmore

13. -

14. W. King

15. Breckinbridge

16. H. Hamlin / A. Johnson

17. -

18. Colfax / Wilson

19. Wheeler

20. C. Arthur

21. -

22. Hendricks

23. Morton

24. Stevenson

25. Hobart / T. Roosevelt

26. Fairbanks

27. Sherman

28. Marshall

29. C. Coolidge

30. Dawes

31. Curtis

32. Garner / Wallace / H. Truman

33. Barkley

34. R. Nixon

35. L.B. Johnson

36. H. Humphrey

37. Agnew / G. Ford

38. N. Rockefeller

39. Mondale

40. G. H.W. Bush

41. D. Quayle

42. A. Gore

43. D. Cheney

44. J. Biden

5.

John F. Kennedy

Lyndon B. Johnson

Richard Nixon

Gerald Ford

Jimmy Carter

Ronald Reagan

George H.W. Bush

Bill Clinton

George W. Bush

Barack Obama

6.

Martha Washington – George

Abigail Adams – John

Martha Jefferson – Thomas (Martha died eighteen years before Thomas Jefferson became president.)

Dolley Madison – James

Elizabeth Monroe – James

Louisa Adams – John Quincy

Rachel Jackson – Andrew (Rachel died three months before Andrew Jackson's inauguration.)

Hannah Van Buren – Martin (She died eighteen years before he became president.)

Anna Harrison – William H.

Letitia Tyler – John

Sarah Polk – James

Margaret Taylor – Zachary

Abigail Fillmore – Millard

Jane Pierce – Franklin

Harriet Lane – James (She was the niece of the president and fulfilled the position of First Lady for her uncle.)

Mary Lincoln – Abraham

Eliza Johnson – Andrew

Julia Grant – Ulysses S.

Lucy Hayes – Rutherford B.

Lucretia Garfield – James

Ellen Arthur – Chester (Ellen died the year before Chester Arthur became president.)

Frances Cleveland – Grover

Caroline Harrison – Benjamin

Frances Cleveland – Grover

Ida McKinley – William

Edith Roosevelt – Theodore

Helen Taft – William

Ellen Wilson – Woodrow and his second wife while in office was Edith Wilson

Florence Harding – Warren

Grace Coolidge – Calvin

Lou Hoover – Herbert

Eleanor Roosevelt – Franklin D.

Bess Truman – Harry

Mamie Eisenhower – Dwight D.

Jackie Kennedy – John F.

Lady Bird Johnson – Lyndon B.

Pat Nixon – Richard

Betty Ford – Gerald

Rosalynn Carter – Jimmy

Nancy Reagan – Ronald

Barbara Bush – George H.W.

Hilary Clinton – Bill

Laura Bush – George W.

Michelle Obama

7. Check list above for answers

8. Answers will vary.

9. Answers will vary.

10. Answers will vary.

11.

1-natural born citizenship

2- 35 years or older

3- must have been a resident within the U.S. at least 14 years

12. Article 2, Section 1 of the United States Constitution

The Constitution is also correct even if you don't know exactly where in the Constitution it can be found.

13. 5

The presidents still alive today (at the time this book was written) are:

Barack Obama

George W. Bush

Bill Clinton

George H.W. Bush

Jimmy Carter

20

Illness, Accidents, and Death

Answers are given at the end of the chapter.

1. Of the first five presidents, how many of them died on the 4th of July?

2. Which president died of acute gastroenteritis after eating cherries, raw vegetables, and milk at a ceremony for the uncompleted Washington Monument?

3. You could actually say this president's lengthy inaugural address is what killed him, since he stood in the outdoors with no hat or coat and ended up with pneumonia and died. Who was he?

4. Which president carried two bullets, from two separate occasions, in his body for years?

5. Which of our presidents was in a wheelchair as a result of polio?

6. Which past president's death went publicly unacknowledged by the acting President Lincoln, because he considered him a traitor to the Union because he had voted in favor of Virginia seceding from the United States?

7. Which president was assassinated after only a few months in office?

8. Which president was shot and hit twice by Lee Harvey Oswald as the president was driving by in a motorcade?

9. Which president had a secret operation due to cancer aboard a yacht in order to keep it a secret from the American public?

10. Which president was on his way to visit his wife, who was suffering from malaria, when he was assassinated?

11. There was an attempted assassination attack on which president's life when he was living at the Blair House due to the White House being under renovation? The assassination attempt failed, and the president was unharmed. Who is he?

12. Which president's dying wish was that one day he would meet

all his friends again on the other side – both white and black friends he emphasized?

13. After which president was shot did Alexander Graham Bell attempt to find the bullet still inside the President by using a metal detector Bell had designed?

14. Which two presidents died on July 4, 1826 – the 50th anniversary of the adoption of the Declaration of Independence?

15. Did John Wilkes Booth act alone in plotting Abraham Lincoln's assassination?

16. Which president during his youth was saved from drowning?

17. Who was the second president to die while in office?

18. Which president was assassinated in Dallas, Texas?

19. Which president's son's body was stolen by grave robbers a short time after his death and sold to a medical school? The school had no idea whose body it was until the president's grandson visited the school on business and discovered his father's body dangling by the neck at the end of a rope. Which president was it?

20. After this president's assassination, Theodore Roosevelt became president. Name the president that was assassinated.

21. Which president's contents from his pocket on the night he was assassinated remained sealed until the year 1976?

22. There was a failed assassination attempt on which president's life in the form of a car bomb in Kuwait?

23. Which president, just two months after his inauguration, survived an assassination attempt? He is the only president to have been shot while in office and survive?

24. Which president suffered a stroke while president?

25. Which president smoked twenty cigars a day and later in life developed mouth cancer?

26. As a teen, what president underwent major surgery and was given only brandy as a sedative?

27. The first assassination attempt on a president was unsuccessful. Who was the president?

28. True or False.

Franklin D. Roosevelt was assassinated in Miami as five shots were fired at him.

29. How many presidents have been assassinated and who are they?

30. After an assassination attempt was made on this president's life, on the way to surgery to remove the bullet he jokingly said, "I forgot to duck." Who was he?

31. True or False.

At the time President Lincoln was assassinated, he was dying of heart disease.

32. Which president is buried in America's largest mausoleum, which was paid for by donations from people worldwide?

33. What disease did John F. Kennedy contract as a young child?

34. John Hinckly, Jr. tried to assassinate this president because of an obsession he had over an actress. He was caught and committed to a mental institution. Which president did he attempt to assassinate?

35. Which president, as an infant, was once presumed dead after suffering from an illness? His parents could find no vital signs and pennies were placed over his eyes and a sheet drawn over his face until his uncle, a doctor, arrived and revived him. Who was he?

36. Who was the first president to be buried in Arlington National Cemetery?

37. It was revealed after his retirement that he had Alzheimers. Who was he?

38. In what city was William McKinley assassinated?

39. Who succeeded to the presidency after President Lincoln was assassinated?

40. Where and how was Abraham Lincoln assassinated?

41. Which president, just a year after becoming president, learned he had a fatal kidney disease?

42. Which president survived an assassination attempt in the 1912 election, when the metal case for his glasses in his pocket stopped a bullet from going through to his heart?

43. Who was the first president to have his funeral broadcast on the radio?

44. Which president was shot on his way to make a speech? He insisted on giving his speech before going to the hospital. The bullet was never removed.

45. Which president requested that at his death his body be wrapped in an American flag with his head resting on a copy of the Constitution?

46. Who was the first president to have an assassination attempt made on his life, but was saved because the gun did not fire properly?

47. Of all the presidents, who lived the longest?

48. How many presidents are buried at The Arlington National Cemetery? Can you name them?

49. Which president had two assassination attempts made on his life, both by women?

50. Which president was buried at Washington National Cathedral, the only president buried in the nation's capital?

51. Which president in his last days as he was dying was offered stimulants to keep him alive until July 4th so he could join three other former presidents to have died on that historic date?

52. Which president died from a heart attack while in office?

Answers

Chapter 20

1. 3

John Adams and Thomas Jefferson both died on July 4th, 1826 and James Monroe died on July 4th, 1831.

2. Zachary Taylor

*Many people were convinced he had been poisoned. His remains were exhumed and their theory was found to be incorrect.

3. William H. Harrison

4. Andrew Jackson

5. Franklin D. Roosevelt

6. John Tyler

7. James Garfield

8. John F. Kennedy

9. Grover Cleveland

10. James Garfield

11. Harry Truman

12. Andrew Jackson

13. James Garfield

*Unfortunately, he was unsuccessful in locating the bullet and the president died from infection and internal hemorrhaging.

14. John Adams and Thomas Jefferson

15. No

16. Ulysses S. Grant

17. Zachary Taylor

*At the time this book was written eight presidents have died in office. They are: William Harrison, Zachary Taylor, Abraham Lincoln, James Garfield, William McKinley, Warren Harding, Franklin D. Roosevelt, and John F. Kennedy. Of those eight, four were assassinated and four died of natural causes.

18. John F. Kennedy

* Bonus question: Who shot and killed Oswald?

Answer: Jack Ruby

19. William Harrison

20. William McKinley

21. Abraham Lincoln

*The contents in his pockets were: two pairs of glasses, a lens cleaner, pocketknife, handkerchief, a watch fob, wallet, Confederate five dollar bill, and a news clipping.

22. George H.W. Bush

23. Ronald Reagan

24. Woodrow Wilson

25. Ulysses S. Grant

26. James Polk

27. Andrew Jackson

28. False.

*The assassination attempt was unsuccessful.

29. 4

Abraham Lincoln, James Garfield, William McKinley, and John F. Kennedy

30. Ronald Reagan

31. True.

*Although he may have been unaware of it. Studying Lincoln's medical history brought doctors to the belief that he was suffering from Marfan's Syndrome.

32. Ulysses S. Grant

33. Scarlet fever

34. Ronald Reagan

35. Herbert Hoover

36. William Taft

37. Ronald Reagan

38. Buffalo, New York

39. Andrew Johnson

40. Ford's Theater. He was shot in the back of his head by John Wilkes Booth.

41. Chester Arthur

42. Theodore Roosevelt

43. William Taft

44. Theodore Roosevelt

45. Andrew Johnson

46. Andrew Jackson

47. Gerald Ford died at ninety-three years of age.

48. 2

*Taft and Kennedy are buried at Arlington National Cemetery

49. Gerald Ford

50. Woodrow Wilson

*While Arlington National Cemetery is just across the Potomac River, it lies in the state of Virginia.

51. James Madison

*He refused.

52. Warren Harding

*It is believed he died of a heart attack, though no autopsy was preformed to prove that fact one way or the other.

Thank you for choosing 'The Big Book of Presidential Trivia.' I hope you enjoyed testing your trivia knowledge about the presidents and maybe even learned something. I would appreciate it if you would take the time to leave feedback to let other readers know what you thought about the book.

If you enjoyed this book of trivia on the presidents, be sure to look for 'The Big Book of First Ladies Trivia.'

Thank you,

Cheryl Pryor

Made in the USA
Middletown, DE
23 March 2016